DECODING THE WELLNESS
MANTRA

ISBN 9781922267597 (print)

Published by Upself in 2021
upself.com.au

Book production by Booktopia Publishing, a division of Booktopia Group Ltd
Unit E1, 3-29 Birnie Avenue
Lidcombe, NSW 2141, Australia
booktopia.com.au

Printed and bound in Australia by SOS Print + Media Group

DECODING THE WELLNESS MANTRA

Tracey Jewel

CONTENTS

Decode

Transitive verb

a: to convert (something, such as a coded message) into intelligible form.

b: to recognise and interpret (an electronic signal)

FOREWORD

Taryn Lee

When your energy vibrates at a frequency that is within direct alignment to what the universe has been attempting to deliver your entire life, you begin to live in the flow and true miracles start to happen.

The universe responds to YOUR personal frequency. Because everything is energy, and the way everything communicates is by emitting frequencies.

That is THE language.

So, the universe does not recognise your desires, wants, or needs, not because it doesn't want to, but simply because it DOESN'T understand them! It only understands the frequency of your vibrations.

This means, if you're vibrating at a frequency of negativity – such as shame or fear – you are going to attract things vibrating at a similar frequency, to support the negative vibrations you're emitting.

The same can be said of the opposite. When you're vibrating the frequency of positivity, such as joy, abundance and love, you are going to attract things that support those positives.

This whole frequency thing has been described as just like tuning a radio.

'You have to be tuned into the radio station you want to listen to, just like you have to be tuned into the energy you want to manifest in your life.'

Never mind what is. Imagine the way you want it to be, so that your vibration matches your desire. When your vibration is a match to your desire, all things in your experience will gravitate to meet that match every time

The trick I've learnt to manifestation. The more I focused on my own energy, my happiness and harmonising my internal world … The more effortless and synchronistic the external manifestations appeared

THE BIGGER PICTURE …

The one thing I've come to realise is that everything always works out if you trust in the bigger picture of your vision.

We've all had those moments when things feel like they are falling apart – love, career, opportunities. But what if every break-up, mistake, missed turn, or even trauma, was actually your course being corrected to exactly where you are meant to be?

What if we trusted that those breaking moments are all part of the bigger picture? That they are part of the vision we were given, and are here to serve us and help us to grow into the best versions of ourselves.

What if it was all falling together – falling together even better than we could have planned or imagined?

Instead of it being the breaking of you, what if you chose those pivotal moments to be the making of a more powerful, more driven, more experienced, more inspired you?

The commonality I see in those who achieve their goals and dreams, is they hold tight to the bigger picture vision and let go of the details. They quickly learn to accept lessons and adapt to failures, frustrations and setbacks.

Yes, they may pivot along the way – maybe change a relationship, a career or an opportunity – but they are always heading towards the one ultimate goal.

Remember this when you're in a hard place or feel like you are really being challenged.

Trust in where you're heading.

Believe in the bigger picture.

Course correct where you need to.

If that big picture vision exists in your heart and in your mind, it is yours to have. It will be your reality.

You are being presented with a choice: Evolve or repeat.

If you choose to remain unchanged, your life with be on repeat. You will be presented with the same challenges, the same routines, the same storms, the same situations, until you learn from them, until you love yourself enough to say 'no more', until you choose change.

If you choose to evolve, you will connect with the strength within you, you will explore what lies outside the comfort zone that's keeping you small, you will awaken to real love, you will become what you came here to be.

Choose to evolve.

I promise, on the other side of that evolution is where your bliss, goals and dreams are waiting for you.

We have come together to create this book with a common purpose. As wellness leaders, we are being called to shift into higher levels of consciousness and lead from a new paradigm: one where we are more connected and can make a greater impact as a combined force. We are so excited to share our soul tribe, energy, joy, purpose, goals and unlimited abundance in the hope and vision you will have the same.

DECODE YOUR CLARITY

INTRODUCTION

Tracey Jewel

There are few things more powerful than
a life lived with passionate clarity.
– Erwin McManus

I've always been a planner, but things haven't always gone to plan! I can look back at the times in my life where I had crystal-clear clarity, times when I could see and feel my vision like it was my current reality. It was at these times I seemed to manifest and align effortlessly.

I've also had a lot of times when I felt like I was living in a fog and was unable to connect with my goals and be present in the day. It's completely normal to experience this entire spectrum.

But I found the key for living my best life was to get myself out of those fog-like states (not stubbornly stick to that space), and get myself back into alignment – without feeling guilty and beating myself up!

To manifest something in your life, you must first clarify the vision of what you want. What does it look like? Feel like? Smell like?

Decoding your own unique clarity paves the way for you to open your mind and heart and begin to imagine the reality of having what you say you want – clarity about your goals, clarity about your past and clarity about your present.

Knowing and being in tune with your goals, aspirations and intentions, and the energy that accompanies them, means you can begin to acknowledge and release the subconscious energy blocks that are holding you back from successfully manifesting what you want.

Vision without action is merely a dream. Action without vision just passes the time. Vision with action can change the world.

A great journaling exercise is to remember a time when you had total clarity about what you wanted and were able to manifest it. Picture a time when you created something from a space of clarity, something that seemed difficult, far-fetched or out of reach, but you did it. Describe what happened, step by step and in as much detail as possible, from start to finish. What did you do? How did you feel? Journal it all. If you did it then, you can duplicate it and do it again and again.In the chapters ahead, are some of my favourite examples of clarity aha-moments, vision crafting and goal setting.

VISION CRAFTING

Lauren Prosser

> Everything is energy and that's all there is to it. Match the frequency of the reality you want and you cannot help but get that reality. It can be no other way. This is not philosophy. This is physics.
>
> – Albert Einstein

What is your vision for your life? Have you actually sat down and thought about this before? Is your current reality a reflection of the kind of life that you wish to be living? Do you get small glimpses of your ideal life while on holiday, and then go back home and grind the rest of your days throughout the year? Do you feel stuck in your current reality? Resigned to thinking that things could be any better?

The thing is … things really could be better. And the best part is, it doesn't need to be hard – something you must hustle to achieve. It can be a process that is fun, and that you enjoy. It is your choice.

Successful people aren't born successful. They are people just like you and me. What makes them stand out from the rest is that they take the time to make a conscious choice. They become crystal clear about exactly what they want to achieve, focus their energy towards achieving it, and commit to working on it consistently until they make it happen.

You are the creator of your life. Every decision, thought, belief and action that you have had in the past has brought you to the point where you are at right now. What is even better is that you can now choose how you wish your reality to be. It is all a vibration. Your vibrational frequency is completely made up of everything you are currently living and experiencing; and your vibrational frequency affects everything you wish to call into your life. You may have big dreams about what you want to achieve in your life, but if you are not a vibrational match for it you won't be able to call it in. You need to raise your frequency and your vibration to match the frequency of what it is you are wanting to call in.

You see, everything is energy and energy is everything. You are a combination of billions of tiny molecules vibrating to a specific frequency. Everything has a vibration and like attracts like. When you are vibrating to a lower frequency everything feels like a challenge. Life doesn't flow. It feels like an uphill battle. A struggle. Difficult situations surround you. You are filled with a lack of sense of self.

When you vibrate at a higher frequency, everything happens with ease. Life is magic. Everything you've ever dreamed of is magnetised to you.

This is where intentional manifestation comes into play. When you become intentional with your life, being crystal clear on the ideal vision of the life that you wish to be living. You can then do the internal work to raise your vibration to match the frequency of your vision in order to make it happen.

In saying this, I'd like to share with you how I have used intentional manifestation to call in my ideal, dream reality …

I'm sure I'm much like you. I have great friends and a wonderful, supportive family. I love life and enjoy investing in my personal growth. That is now, but I wasn't always who I pride myself on being today.

Growing up I was a very shy and insecure young girl. I hated being in photos. I was afraid to speak up and be seen. In group situations, I was incredibly awkward because I was so intimidated by everyone else. When I was presented with an opportunity to step-up, I would shy away out of a fear of not being good enough and thinking someone else would be better. Deep down inside, though, whenever I said no to myself, I would feel a dagger stab me in the heart. I knew I wanted to be more, and so I began to work on myself to make this happen.

I've spent many years doing personal development, peeling back the layers of insecurities and fears; now the new modalities that I'm working with have accelerated things even further. These days, I no longer hold myself back. I look fear in the eye, and I give it a wink!

I am so grateful to now feel confident – to be the happy, positive person I truly am. I am driven to succeed, and I step up to the plate, time and time again. I have achieved massive success in all areas of my life. I love my life and those I get to share it with. I am in a wonderful, loving relationship with my husband, and we have three beautiful, cheeky little children together. We have just bought our first family home, and we're excited at the prospect of building upon it and making it our dream, forever home – setting down some solid roots and building a strong foundation for our family and our children's upbringing.

I feel good in my own skin and I like what I see in the mirror. I love learning and study different courses on health, fitness, lifestyle, mindset, alternative healing modalities and all things related to spirituality. And I'm always wanting to learn more and more, not only to help me be the best person that I can be, but also so I can help my clients on a deeper level.

I am now an author, and I am doing my dream work of speaking on stage. The work that I do lights me up and gives me a sense of purpose, as I know I have a positive impact on the lives of those I get to work with.

I am a role model and mentor for those who are just like the girl I was all those years ago: women who are shy and insecure, who feel unworthy and not good enough, but who deep inside have a burning desire to be something more! I now get to help them shift what is holding them back so they can unlock their full potential and live their ultimate lives.

I have achieved everything I dreamed of when I crafted my last life vision five years ago. I am living proof that when you become intentional with your life, you really can call in everything you've ever dreamed of. Now, I get to share my favourite tried and tested ways of intentional manifestation and vision crafting with you.

Vision Crafting

What does your most abundant life look like?

What would be going on for you?

Ask yourself these question as you reflect upon every area of your life:

- romance
- family and friends
- health and fitness
- abundance
- purpose
- passion and fun
- contribution
- spirituality
- learning and growth

Close your eyes and tap into the feelings of having already achieved abundant life. Feel all of the emotions and the feelings, hear the sounds, see the visuals, taste the tastes. Allow your body to feel all the senses as you connect with your vision.

Focus on where you'd like to be in the next two to five years. Consider your age at that point and you'll get an instant visual. This will help you to connect to the life vision you're intending to manifest.

This process may sound simple, but it's incredibly powerful! Even elite athletes do this before they run a race. It's been scientifically proven that when you visualise a scenario in your mind, the same neurons fire in your brain as if it was actually happening. You are able to connect with the frequency of having already achieved this outcome. Therefore, by raising your vibration to match this reality, you will ultimately be able to magically manifest it into your life.

So, now that you have a crystal-clear image of the ideal reality you wish to be living in every area of your life, I want you to get a pen and paper and write out this vision into a statement.

Key points:

- Write in present tense. For example, 'I am so happy and grateful that …'
- Make it something you feel inspired by. Infuse it with passion.
- Don't let not having enough money, skills or time hold you back.
- Focus on what you'd ultimately love to do, rather than being frustrated with what you are currently doing.
- Put aside any limitations. Dream big and focus on success.
- Describe how you feel and the type of qualities you now embody.
- Align it with your passions, values and goals.

Pro tips to help accelerate the process:

- Save your life vision in the notes in your phone. Whenever you have a spare moment throughout your day read over your vision. Close your eyes and connect with it. Visualise that it is already done. Feel all of the feelings and emotions of having already achieved it. Tap into the frequency that it's already done. The more you tap into it, the more you raise your frequency to the vibration of what it is you're wishing to call in, and the sooner it will happen.
- Write out your vision on a piece of paper and put it on your mirror in your bathroom, so that every time you go to the bathroom you are reminded to connect to your vision. As you wash your hands, close your eyes and visualise your life vision.
- Create a vision board. Cut out pictures of everything you wish to call in. Spend time every day connecting with it. Close your eyes and visualise yourself living that reality.
- Throughout your day, notice all of the small shifts that are occurring in your life that are aligned to your vision and the life that you are calling in. Perhaps you get offered an opportunity, or someone links you up with someone who is able to help you achieve your goal. Spend some time each day reflecting upon these events, acknowledging how amazing it is that these events have happened and smiling to yourself as you pat yourself on the back for your efforts. Having this awareness helps cement these progressions into your conscious mind. By focusing on these small wins and celebrating them, with deliberate and focused attention, you are able to raise your frequency and magnetise more opportunities that are of a similar vibration into your life.

- If you can, incorporate frequency healing into your daily practice. By doing this, it raises your frequency, as you use individualised frequencies to help balance your mind and body and to relieve stress. In this way, your vibration will be more aligned with what it is you're wishing to call in, magnetising everything to you and accelerating the manifestation process.
- If you really want to accelerate the manifestation process even faster do breathwork and movement. Find someone who can guide you through it safely. Breathwork and movement helps shift and rewire your entire system. Releasing what is holding you back, so that you can unlock your full potential and accelerate the manifestation process.
- Invest in a coach or a mentor. Someone who has already achieved the results you're after and can show you how they did it. That will shortcut the process and avoid spending years doing trial and error like I did initially.

If there is any way I can help you to release whatever is holding you back so that you can begin living life as the happiest, healthiest, and fittest version of you, then please feel free to reach out … I'm sure we could create some magic together.

And remember…

> You are stronger than you think, powerful beyond belief, and more capable than you imagine. It's your time now!
> – Lauren Prosser

Lauren Prosser

Lauren has achieved her dream of becoming a highly accredited physical activator, wellness life coach and quantum healing practitioner.

She has impacted many lives using unique mindset rewiring tools, powerful breathwork and movement processes and transformational healing techniques, and now she wants to help you too.

She will disrupt your version of normal, and help you break free of old, archaic systems. She will use the most potent modalities she works with to help you shift what is holding you back in your current reality, creating instant, life-changing results.

Lauren's passion is in helping women achieve their best lives, living fearlessly into their purpose and unlocking their greatness.

Her specialty is in helping regular, everyday women remove whatever is holding them back from stepping into their full potential, so that they can begin to live the life they know they were meant to live.

Work with Lauren:

Lauren is currently working with clients one-to-one and in group settings, both online and in person at retreats and workshops.

Her specialty is creating bespoke mind body soul transformation programs, helping women overcome past traumas, fears and self-doubts, and empowering them to live life as the happiest, healthiest and fittest version of themselves possible.

Special Offer:

10% off any current signature offer, plus a free 15-minute discovery call.

Website: www.laurenprosser.com
Email: lauren@laurenprosser.com
Instagram: @laurenprosser
Facebook: www.facebook.com/laurenprossercoach
LinkedIn: www.linkedin.com/in/lauren-prosser/

GOAL SETTING WITH PURPOSE AND PASSION

Kathryn Beacroft

The big secret in life is there is no secret.
Whatever your goal. You can get
there if you're willing to work.

– Oprah Winfrey

I think goal setting is one of the most important activities you can undertake to really focus your life and feel as if you are aligned with your life's purpose.

Where do you sit currently with goal setting? Are you going well with goal setting? Or do you need some steps, tools and techniques to help you set some goals in your life?

Do you already use goal setting in your life? Have you set goals before – however big or small – and successfully achieved them? Or is goal setting something you have tried, but it didn't work so you left it for those people who succeed at everything they do?

Which of the following two scenarios best describes your approach to goal setting?

SCENARIO 1

You set a goal you were so excited about that you thought about it every day.

You visualised yourself achieving that goal.

You told family and friends about your goal.

You dreamed about it.

You could see and feel yourself achieving that goal.

You believed 100 per cent in yourself that you would achieve that goal.

You would not let anything prevent you from achieving that goal.

Can you think of a time in your life that you did this?

SCENARIO 2

You had a time when you thought it would be so nice to have a lot more money in your bank account – maybe several thousand or even a million dollars – but then you thought:

That's never going to happen.

Only rich people make that sort of money.

I am not one of those people.

I can't do that.

No one in my family has ever made that much money.

I will never have that much money in my bank.

Let's assess the two scenarios. What are the main differences between them?

In the first scenario, you set a goal and you 100 per cent believed you would achieve it. You applied all the skills of a goal setter, maybe without even realising it, and I would say you most probably achieved your goal, or very close to it.

In the second scenario, you had a goal – or a brief wish – and thought it would be nice to have more money. But you did not get very specific about your goal, and you let your mind talk you out of it. You did not use any goal setting techniques to bring this wish into a reality.

Can you see where in your life either of these types of behaviour have occurred before? And what were the results?

We know that athletes training for an event such as the Olympics will use a very strict process of goal setting to achieve their goal of winning a medal. There have been many athletes who have overcome extreme challenges to win in their chosen sport, as that was their goal, their dream, their passion and their purpose.

Did the famous and successful people you know just wake up one day already successful, popular and earning millions of dollars?

No of course they didn't. They had to:

- plan their goals
- plan their lives
- plan their journey to success.

Did they have any failures, setbacks, knockbacks?

If you read about their stories, you will find most successful people have had to overcome one if not several adversities to get to where they are.

I am going to share with you some keys tools and techniques that are used worldwide by some of the most successful people in the world – tools and techniques you can apply in your life moving forward to set goals, find your passion and find your purpose.

First, I would love to share with you how I became so excited about goal setting and mindset.

I was at my first ever personal development event. I didn't know what to expect, but I soon discovered that mindset was one of the most inspiring things I had ever learnt about.

On the last day of the event, we were given an exercise which was a turning point in my life – a point from which I knew I was never going back to the old me again. I was in a room of about 500 people, and we were each given a candle. The presenters explained they would turn all the lights out and then light one candle only. That candle would then be used to light another candle, and so on. Every person who had a lit candle could light the candle of someone near to them, until all the candles in the room were lit.

It was surreal watching all 500 candles being lit, one by one, from that initial flame in a matter of minutes. It was so fast.

The presenters then read to us the famous passage written by Marianne Williamson in her book *Return to Love*. The sentences I will always remember are:

'Our deepest fear is not that we are inadequate. Our deepest fear is that we are powerful beyond measure … As we let our own light shine, we give others permission to do the same.'

This experience made me realise the power of every individual having a unique purpose to bring to the world and living that purpose.

Now the fun begins. It's your turn to set some goals. Let's set some goals together.

STEP 1 – What is it you would really like to be doing?

To answer this question, I would like you to take a few calming breaths – in and out – and maybe even shut your eyes and tune into you. Ask yourself what it is you would really like to do.

> Put your hand on your heart and ask yourself, what do I want? The first thing that comes to mind is always the right one. – Layne Beachley (surfing world champion)

If you tune in and listen, in your heart you usually know the answer. If the answer does not come immediately, try this tuning in exercise over a few days – preferably when you are calm and relaxed. Maybe even go to a peaceful place where you can sit and meditate, such as the beach or a park.

Once you have an answer, the fun begins – bringing your goals to reality! Does that sound exciting? Let's get started.

STEP 2 – Write out your goal in detail

Write out your goal in as much detail as possible.

What exactly is your goal?

- When you would like to achieve this goal by? Three months? Six months? Five years?
- How many people will this impact (approximately)?
- How much money do you expect to make (approximately and if relevant)?

Now write this goal as a statement you can read every morning, setting the scene in the future and seeing yourself having achieved your goal. For example:

It is 31 December 202X. I am celebrating my incredible success in achieving my goal of ________________________. I am so happy and grateful for my life, for my friends and for everyone who has worked with me towards achieving this goal.

Thank you, thank you, thank you.

STEP 3 – Identify your WHY

The next really important step is to identify why this goal is important to you. Identifying your WHY will help to keep you on track if things start to get in your way.

Sometimes it may seem like the universe is testing you, as if to say: How bad do you really want this? Are you willing to really put in the effort required?

Once you have identified your WHY, read it every day when you read your goal.

STEP 4 – Commit to your goal

The next step is to 100 per cent commit to your goal and not let anything get in your way.

Have you heard the saying 'let's burn the boats'? This quote literally means if you travel across the water to an island and you then burn the boats, there is no going back. This concept of burning boats traces back to 1519, when Hernán Cortés led a large expedition – 600 Spaniards in eleven ships – to Mexico. He commanded his men to burn all the ships as there was no going back.

So, when you set a goal, commitment to the goal is very important. And if you remember this analogy of burning the boats, that is what is required – 100 per cent commitment, and no turning back.

STEP 5 – Break your goal into small steps

The next step in bringing your purpose and passion to the world is to break your goals into small steps – small achievable chunks. Then set up your plan for the week and the month with three daily actions you can achieve to keep moving forward towards your goal.

First make a list of everything you can think of that you need to do to achieve the goal – you can always add to this list. The key is to write down everything in your mind at that moment and to immediately get started (give yourself about thirty minutes to one hour to do this).

Now organise that list into what needs to be done first, and so on. For example, first may be to:

- Seek some professional guidance.
- Do some research into your topic.
- Seek out partners.
- Attend a course that will help you with the skills you need.

Every day set yourself the next three steps you need to take to achieve your goal.

> The most difficult thing is the decision to act. The rest is merely tenacity. – Amelia Earhart

You may not be able to complete those three steps each day, so carry over what you don't complete to the next day.

STEP 6 – Celebrate your success

The final and really important part of goal setting is to celebrate your success – however small it is. Do not wait for the day you finally achieve your goal. Celebrate every win along the way, however big or small.

I use a 'daily success journal', where each day I write down every small step I take towards my goals. For example, I write down if I go to the gym, create a blog post, eat an apple instead of a chocolate bar, and so on.

The reason I love this practice of celebrating every action I take towards achieving my goal is that you start to see all the little actions as positive steps towards your goal, instead of looking at your day in terms of all the things you haven't finished, all the things you still have to do.

It's like giving yourself gold stars. We all know how much our brain prefers rewards to punishments. Celebrating my successes is part of my daily routine, and I love it! I am sure you will love this too, and you will find how powerful this small practice is.

STEP 7 – Gratitude

This is an important step in goal setting as it helps to keep you in a positive state. Even when things may not seem to be going according to plan, if you start and end the day in a state of gratitude you will find your day will flow more easily.

I love to write three things in my journal every morning and every night that I am grateful for and why. This reminds me every day of all the wonderful blessings in my life, and starts and ends my day in a state of gratitude – a powerful, energetic state to be in.

Even though life may throw you a curved ball, looking for things to be grateful for can help shift your focus from the negative to the positive. There are so many things to be grateful for – the beautiful blue sky, the birds in the trees, the sun that shines, books to read – the list is endless.

Once you start this practice, you will start to see how many amazing things you have to be grateful for every day. Try it. I am sure you will love this daily practice.

STEP 8 – Just start

Congratulations! You have the eight key steps. You are ready to set some amazing goals with purpose and passion, so all you need to do is start. I love this quote by Mel Robbins, author of *The 5 Second Rule.*

> Start now. Start where you are. Start with fear. Start with pain. Start with doubt. Start with your hands shaking. Just start. – Mel Robbins

I believe goal setting – having a goal bigger than you, a goal or purpose that can directly benefit you and may also benefit others – is the ultimate key to happiness in life.

Please keep us updated by letting us know the amazing goals you have set and what you have achieved.

And remember …

You are supported by the universe, and you can always reach out to any of the amazing authors of this book for support – we are all here for you!

You have a unique purpose to bring to the world. Shine your light bright, beautiful one!

With so much love and gratitude to you always. xxxx

Kathryn Beacroft

Kathryn was a successful accountant for ten years and then realised that was not her purpose. She retrained as a naturopath, nutritionist and transformational mindset coach. She has over twelve years of experience as a health and wellness practitioner. During this time she has seen over 10,000 clients.

Kathryn loves coaching her clients to follow their true passion and purpose and to achieve optimal health in both BODY and MIND. She would love to help you find out what truly excites and inspires you.

Kathryn is the creator of 28THRIVE, an online program that supports you on your journey to transform your MIND – BODY – LIFE!

Please download your FREE copy of Kathryn's ebook – *4 Keys to Find Your Purpose.*

Website: www.bhealth.net.au

Instagram: _bhealth_

Facebook: www.facebook.com/KathrynBeacroftOfficial

LinkedIn: www.linkedin.com/in/kathrynbeacroft777

DECODING THE FOUNDATION OF WORTHINESS

Caroline Watson

You deserve to be seen, you deserve to be heard, you deserve to feel vibrant and you deserve to feel safe. Not because of what you have, or haven't done, but because everyone does. And you're not an exception to that. You're NOT less than anyone else.

– Caroline Watson

I wrote that recently to my twenty-four-year-old self from the perspective of forty-four-year-old me. A lot can change in twenty years!

You see, I grew up in a very conservative, religious household in rural South Australia and was taught from an early age to put my trust in powers outside of myself, that the ordained authorities knew best and that questioning or stepping outside the agreed order of things would be greeted with punishment, scorn or abandonment. This extended to me believing that my father, as the head of the household, knew more about who I was, how I functioned, and what was best for me, than I did.

I relinquished my own knowing in favour of what he stated were my personality traits, what was acceptable behaviour, what I should study and what career path to choose. I was incredibly intelligent as a child, winning numerous school prizes, excelling academically (in the top 5 per cent in national academic competitions and achieving high distinctions in my first year of a commerce degree at university with little effort). However, in the ways of the world I was woefully underprepared.

Towards the end of my first year of university, after rebellion against years of blind compliance and experiencing my new-found taste of city life and freedom, I discovered I was pregnant at just nineteen years old. While I sensed a profound love for my unborn daughter, I was convinced I was being punished for being immoral and that the only way to atone for my errant, sinful ways was to marry. Deep down I knew I was choosing a joyless and difficult path, and as I walked down the aisle, the whole of my body was crying out 'Nooooo'. But at that point I didn't feel worthy of anything more. In my eyes, I was now failed, damaged goods and had to live the consequences of my actions. So, I went through the motions.

I spent the next ten years in a haze of blame, shame, regret, guilt, depression, fatigue, frustration and anger. I was angry at the world, at myself and, especially, at my husband, who drank us into bankruptcy while I enabled it. I believed I was stuck and didn't deserve any better. I thought I had to somehow earn my freedom and happiness, but I was at a loss as to how to even start. I second-guessed myself at every turn and constantly feared making more wrong decisions.

One afternoon, I was crying to my grandma after having separated from my husband over the

bankruptcy. Her simple words still echo loud and clear, years after her passing: 'Never give your power away again, my dear.'

It took me another few years, and a second, failed attempt at squeezing myself into that ill-fitting marriage, to truly get the meaning behind those words. But my grandmother had planted a magical seed.

After I finally divorced, I received a ticket to a free day-long seminar. It was all a bit hyped up and reminiscent of the evangelical churches of my childhood, but the one gold nugget I received from it was that I got really clear on what I was asking – I was asking to be able to trust the universe.

Well, that one request opened up a door to more and more possibilities that continued to show up and become greater every day. Shortly afterwards, I discovered the life-changing tools of Access Consciousness® and the mantra: 'All of life comes to me, with ease, joy and glory.'®

A dear friend 'ran my bars' for fifteen minutes and suggested I try saying the mantra daily, ten times in the morning and ten times in the evening, and see what it created. At first it felt like I was lying to myself! I persisted, and the changes were so dramatic that I took an Access Bars class within a fortnight.

Bit by bit, the emotional charge around traumatic memories dissipated, the persistent knot of anxiety in my stomach gradually disappeared, the way I thought things 'had to be' became way less rigid and so many other options popped into my awareness. The negative voices in my head telling me I wasn't good enough, smart enough, strong enough or pretty enough just gradually silenced. Behaviours and comments from others that used to trigger me just didn't push my buttons anymore. I no longer road-raged!

My relationships with my children, new partner (now husband) and workmates became more fun and I laughed a whole lot more often. My mind was clearer and my ability to just go with the flow, instead of having to control everything, grew exponentially.

Several years later (after completing an environmental science degree) I became an Access Bars Facilitator to create an even greater wave of empowerment and joy rippling out into the world. Over time, choosing my way, step by step, out of the heavy weight of my limiting beliefs and conditioning, I came to realise that I AM the universe – the drop in the ocean AND the ocean, all at once. I do the choosing, I do the creating, I now trust ME and, in doing so, trust the universe. And, since I am the universe, I am worthy of receiving love, compassion and abundance.

Most people think and believe that change has to be hard-fought, messy, painful, drama-filled or bring tears, and that each issue has to be brought to the conscious level one by one to be dealt with, when the truth and reality is that (though still uncomfortable at times) it can actually be quite fast, easy and broad spectrum! So much so, that the most difficult part for me sometimes is actually acknowledging how much has changed over these past few years!

I can now stand in a circle of people from all walks of life and remain energetically expanded thanks to knowing I am equal to any one of them: not greater than, not less than, but distinctive and unique with my own place (like any other element in an ecosystem), and equally worthy of ease, joy and abundance.

A healthy cycle of gifting and receiving in life resembles an ebb and flow like the tides. Sometimes we're the giver, sometimes the receiver, with time and space to replenish resources, power and strength in between. This can be difficult to implement if we have a diminished sense of worthiness.

However, we need to reconsider the concept of worthiness. If we come from a background where we weren't listened to or our awareness wasn't valued, it can be a natural response to seek endorsement and approval from others (external validation), or to feel that we are never going to be as valuable or worthy as others. But does a bird deserve to eat? Or does it just receive from nature because it exists? Do we deserve to breathe? Or do we just receive air by virtue of simply being alive? What if you were also already worthy of receiving safety, respect, abundance, joy, health, vitality not because someone decides whether or not you deserve it but simply because you exist?

Re-claiming that knowledge of intrinsic worthiness has been the key to unlocking the true power of me and the foundation to creating and receiving my joy-filled life. And also for you, if you choose it.

Daily Practices

Brag Buddy

Find yourself one trusted person, who truly has your back, to invite to be your brag buddy.

Ask for permission to share the joy of your successes with them, and ask them to remind you that you are worthy of receiving those success and to celebrate. (If you don't yet have this person, ask for them to show up, and in the meantime use a journal.)

Expansion and Receiving Exercise

A free recorded expansion and receiving meditation can be downloaded at: https://thrivingpossibilities.com.au/shop/expansion-exercise/

Tools for Opening up to More of You

These are a few of my favourite Access Consciousness® tools to play with. These and more are covered in more detail in an Access Bars® class.

1. All of life comes to me with ease, joy and glory®

This is the mantra of Access Consciousness®. Experiment with it by saying it to yourself daily for at least a few weeks. Repeat a minimum of ten times in the morning and ten times at night – or even 100 times! You can say it out loud or in your head, depending on your location and audience.

2. Interesting point of view

This is another amazing tool from Access Consciousness®. It is especially useful if you have a tendency to favour other people's awareness over your own. When you notice yourself reacting, resisting, aligning or agreeing to a thought or a comment, just think to yourself 'interesting point of view'. This frees us from having to put something in either the 'right' box or the 'wrong' box and allows it to just float on by as 'interesting'.

3. Light and heavy tool

As illustrated in the Hawkins Consciousness scale in Figure 1 below, ultimate consciousness is a highly expanded state corresponding with joy, peace and enlightenment.

Ultimate consciousness is the state where you are truly being you. What you perceive as light, expansive, joyful is true for you. What you perceive as heavy, dense, contracted is a lie for you. Dropping into your body and sensing that – expansion vs contraction – will enable you to know what's true for you. Follow that awareness with choosing what creates that lightness– if that's the kind of life you would like to create. Bodies never lie.

Be your own scientist and experiment with this. Use it for choosing food, clothes, the drive home and see what it creates. As you use it more and more it's like calibrating and it will become quicker and easier until it's suddenly your natural way of being and choosing.

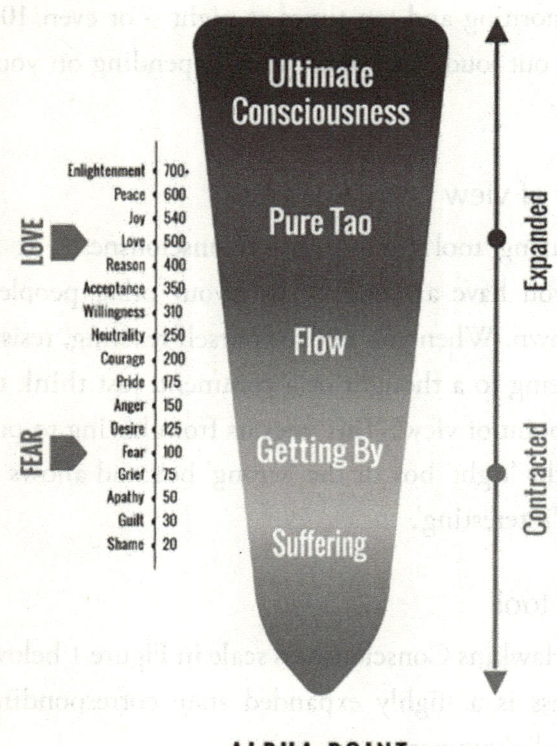

Figure 1. Scale of consciousness from Power vs Force by David Hawkins.

Takeaway

Reclaiming, acknowledging and owning our intrinsic worthiness is the foundation for self-empowerment and for creating and receiving more ease and joy in life. Destroying, uncreating and undoing any conditioning that has us believing that we are somehow 'less than' is the first step to choosing and creating better.

Remember:

- Change can be fast and can happen with ease, it doesn't require force.
- Choose what is light and joyful for you (as that's what is true for you and is also the power of you).
- You are the creator of your reality, your universe – trust you.
- You are worthy.

Caroline Watson

Caroline Watson is a global energetic healer and the creator of Thriving Possibilities.

Caroline was born and raised in rural South Australia. As a child, she a had natural affinity to nature and a profound energetic connection to both animals and the earth. This was not valued at the time and, as a result, Caroline began her career in commerce and financial services. A stint volunteering on a local bushcare site led to her re-connecting with her love of the natural environment, studying conservation and moving to Queensland to work as a biodiversity facilitator for the Australian Government. In 2016 she graduated with a Bachelor of Environmental Science from Charles Darwin

University and worked as an environmental officer/project supervisor within private industry.

During 2012 and 2013, a series of personal challenges and a heavy workload led to physical and emotional burnout. Caroline utilised this opportunity to dramatically transform her worldview, which resulted in her reconnection with her natural awareness of subtle energies and her advanced energetic capabilities.

Caroline is the mother of three children in a blended family and uses her experience as both mother and wife to demonstrate to her clients how her modalities can be applied to create a thriving family life through a myriad of changes. She also applies her broad set of skills, abilities and diverse lived experience to assist individuals to thrive in whatever area of life they would like to create change.

Caroline's approach to her healing modalities is profoundly empowering and encouraging. Her clients leave with a sense that a distinct shift has occurred and new pathways opened with little to no resistance felt by the client as a result of her application of Access Consciousness Bars®, Access Energetic Facelift and Access Body Processes.

During her work in environmental restoration, Caroline noticed a link between the clearing of weeds with a brush-cutter in nature, and the outcome for clients through energy clearing during her use of Pellowah and reiki. It is this beautiful connection to the cycles of growth in nature, that makes her sessions particularly effective at opening up time and space for the client's own personal growth.

Caroline is currently based in the beautiful bayside area of Brisbane (Meanjin). Sessions are also available online and classes are available anywhere in Australia.

Special offer:

Contact Caroline for a 25% discount on your first session or package.

Website: www.thrivingpossibilities.com.au
Instagram: https://www.instagram.com/thrivingpossibilities/
Facebook: https://www.facebook.com/carolinemwatson33/
Linkedlin: www.linkedin.com/in/carolinemwatson33

DECODE YOUR SHADOWS

INTRODUCTION

Tracey Jewel

To light a candle is to cast a shadow.
– Ursula K Le Guin

I ignored my shadow side for a long time, but I always knew what it was. I called her 'Shiny Tracey'. She was the identity I put on when I felt too vulnerable to show my underbelly. She came out when I felt unsafe or didn't want to acknowledge the truth or the parts I had disowned.

Admitting there were parts of myself I didn't like or didn't want a bar of was a hard process. My love for validation, my deepest fear of rejection, keeping people at arm's length, jumping from one toxic relationship to another, being a chameleon, suffering from imposter syndrome – these shadows weren't going away no matter how 'shiny' I got. In fact, it resulted in too much shiny forehead botox! Being radically honest about who you are and what you want is one way you can elevate your vibrational energy and move forward in life. I realised I would keep going round and round in circles unless I made the shadow shift. I had to take a closer look at those places. I needed to identify any negative emotions, triggers and past haunts, and undertake some heavy and deep self-honesty.

The shadow, a concept coined by renowned psychologist Carl Jung, is (in simplest terms) the dark side of the personality. We are comfortable knowing and expressing the lovely, bright, shiny parts of our personalities to the world (think kindness, generosity, and so on), yet we neglect to acknowledge or show our darker shadow side in fear of what society deems unsavoury.

How Does Your Shadow Come into Existence?

No matter how healthy or positive our childhood, we are all bound to experience invalidation at some point. For example, say you displayed a character trait such as rage when you were a toddler, and one of your parents shamed you for it. You would then infer:

> *When I show these parts of myself to the world, I am less lovable. I am less safe. Therefore, it is not safe to show these parts of myself to the world. These parts are less lovable than the rest of me.*

When this occurs, we cast these traits aside into the discard pile of our own personal shadow. Compounded over the years, we deem certain parts of ourselves as 'wrong' or 'unlovable.' The longer we suffocate these parts of ourselves, the more power these traits gain over us while lurking in the shadows of our subconscious mind. These traits that we reject are what form the building blocks of our shadow self.A word about shadows: you don't need to fall apart in shadow work to come together. You're not broken. You can enjoy being in the sun, getting some vitamin D but still casting a shadow on the ground. You can start to connect with the disowned parts of you, without it being a pity party or a negative experience.

Explore the following chapters with an open heart and mind and embrace the shadows to get to a higher light.

THE GIFT OF BEING DIFFERENT

~ And never giving up on YOU! ~

Sarah Andros

One of the things I grew up believing was the importance of 'fitting in'. Much of my childhood and early teens I spent trying to be just like others – striving to wear the 'right' clothes, talking about the things that mattered to others and making sure I knew the storyline of all the popular TV shows. Is any of this familiar to you?

Determined to find the pathway to happiness and a deeper sense of purpose after high school, I chose psychology as my major at university. However, I struggled to find how it made any sense at times, as many of the lecturers themselves had not left the educational institution in decades. They seemed stuck, unhappy, and their textbook knowledge was not satisfying my quest for a sense of purpose.

So, at the age of twenty, having successfully graduated from university, I took off on the adventure of a lifetime and bought a one-way ticket via Singapore and Egypt to Europe. I travelled solo for eighteen months, adventuring, following my instincts and learning to trust my inner knowing.

It was perhaps one of the first times I did not follow what others were doing, and this matched the words of the Robert Frost poem – I was taking the road less travelled. So the quest began to find 'ME' and to create my reality. And it was both during and after these travels that I realised the gift of being different, and to never, ever give up on myself – no matter what!!

On returning to Perth, Western Australia, I was a very different person and was looking on the world with new eyes. The only problem was, those around me had not changed, which highlighted even more that any attempt to fit in would be entirely futile. I had to be willing to be different and make new choices.

A NEW JOURNEY OF DISCOVERY BEGINS

Not long after my return I was diagnosed with debilitating chronic fatigue following glandular fever. And so began a NEW journey of discovery: getting to know and listen to my body, trust my awareness even more, and go within for my answers to getting well. It was such a gift.

Many would say 'that's terrible'. And, of course, at the time it really was not so much fun. However, it catapulted me into a journey of self-discovery at a young age. Since then I have taken many different personal development courses and practitioner training courses, from reiki in my early twenties to Access Consciousness® in my forties (and everything else in between!), and I have never, ever looked back.

I finally started to look at what truly mattered to me and what I valued, so that I could create my reality rather than just fit in. What is YOUR reality? So many of us are looking for our 'purpose', however this is more of a mental construct and very limiting.

What if the true purpose of life is to be HAPPY … and to know that our greatest gift is to acknowledge and embrace the difference we are. We then become a potency that actually manipulates the molecules around us to a degree that the world transforms itself to us and our requests.

The secret to creating a FULFILLED life of EASE and JOY and GLORY is through the willingness to truly create a life that works for us.

It takes courage. And tenacity. And a willingness to sometimes fall apart in order to fall together.

How often have you asked for something and it seems like roadblocks continually show up to 'stop' you?

How often have you stopped moving forward because you allowed the roadblocks to be greater than you?

OVERCOMING BLOCKS & LIMITATIONS

Life itself is a series of sudden turns, bumpy rides, sometimes smooth sailing and everything else in between. There is no denying this to be the case.

The key to success and to an enjoyable life is not in the avoidance of the roadblocks, rather the ways in which we both view and handle them.

The reality is, if we were satisfied with an ordinary life, we may not have to deal with too many roadblocks. We would just live a bland, beige life, with a recurring theme of mediocrity.

Let us not confuse a 'block' with trauma and drama. We tend to create drama and problems if we are not creating enough that we value in life, not choosing things that are congruent, or not showing up as the greatest version of ourselves.

A 'roadblock' is different. It usually indicates something we have to look at or change or address in order to achieve and or receive what we have been asking for. It is the thing that we have allowed to stop or distract us…

In committing to a 'bigger' life, one in which we challenge ourselves to continually be greater, we must learn the ways to flow with, rather than fight against, the ups and downs of life.

CHOOSING GREATER TAKES COURAGE

The universe works in weird and wonderful ways. When we ask for something different to show up, we have to realise several things.

First, things do not always show up as we expect them to. We cannot control the outcome …

Think back to a time when you asked for something. Perhaps it was for a new relationship, or a change in career path, or a move to a different home. How often did this request show up in a way you could not have planned?

The universe desires to give to us, and usually more than we have asked for. What if we were willing to let go and listen to the energetic whispers of the future?

In seeing life from this perspective, we may see that sometimes roadblocks are actually gifts the universe is attempting to give us. When we are able to get beyond our own conclusions, we may begin to see that sometimes what first appears as a problem or a block is actually a blessing in disguise.

It is indeed our perspective that allows us to navigate life with greater ease. When we are able to get out of our own way, we are able to receive things from the universe that do not match our initial expectations. In so doing, we are able to broadband our receiving and go beyond our limited thinking mind.

THE ART OF CHOOSING GREATER

When we are choosing greater in life, anything that has previously stopped us choosing this will often rear its ugly head. (These are all things that can be changed both quickly and simply using the incredible tools of Access Consciousness® that have guided and supported me in my life for the last decade. More on this later.)

Unless we are able to see things from an eyes wide open perspective, we may otherwise view these roadblocks or challenges as a reason to give up or not follow through on creating or achieving our target.

It is a bit like the analogy of the gold digger. The target is to find gold. The digging may have taken days or even weeks. It takes a level of determination to not give up when the going gets tough – when the weather suddenly turns, when the shovel hits an extraordinarily tough band of rocks or when the digger's physical strength starts to give out.

And yet that elusive gold may be sitting only twenty centimetres away. Perhaps another hour of digging would reveal the treasure. If we allow any of these apparent 'roadblocks' to stop us, we may never achieve our desires and reach the gold!

The same is true when we are asking for something more in life. To grow our business, to achieve more sales, to increase our fitness or to reach a new health target.

Anything and everything that has previously stopped, distracted or dissuaded us from actualising this request previously may show up for clearing. It may be a limited perspective or fixed point of view, a doubt or concern, a sense of not being good enough or a lack of trust in ourselves.

When these things surface, this may be the sign of us actually getting closer to what we have asked for. It usually indicates that we are on the pathway to something greater, and that in order to achieve this next step, we must navigate these 'hurdles' and grow new muscles or challenge an old mindset.

Without the tenacity to keep going, many of us give up, request less or settle for something that is not enough for us. We make the block or limitation greater and bigger than us. And we allow ourselves to be stopped.

NEVER GIVING UP ON YOU

The only person who can stop us is US. When we finally get to realise this, we will never see ANYTHING as a roadblock. Rather we will be able to see a roadblock as a gift, and use it to propel us forward and inspire and motivate us to keep going.

What are some of the blocks or limitations you have been functioning from?

What if you were courageous and honest enough to look at these limitations, not from a place of judgement, rather from a place of curiosity?

THE GETTING CLEAR TOOL

Take a few moments now to make a list. Actually, make two lists. Do it now.

In the **first** list write down at least ten things you have been desiring to create or achieve. They could be as simple as: to have more ease in your relationships, to enjoy your body more, or to be open to new possibilities with money.

In the **second** list write down anything you have allowed to stop you creating these things. It may be points of view, a person (perhaps kids or partner), a judgement or a concern.

Once you have made your two lists do the following:

Take the **first** list into your hands, read what is written below out loud then close your eyes.

> Everything that does not allow me to perceive, know, be and receive what is real and true for me I now let it all go. Everything that does not allow me to connect to the energy of my true life I let that go.

Open your eyes and take a look at that first list again. From this more energetic perspective, ask yourself how much of what you have written is true for you; how much of what you have written is congruent with the energy of your true life. You may discover that some of it is based on someone else's projections or expectations of you, or what you have decided is correct. Cross out those things. Only circle the things that light you up.

Now hold the **second** list in your hand, read what is written below out loud then close your eyes:

> How much of what I have written here is true and real for me? How many of these blocks and limitations have I made real and true that are not?

Open your eyes and glance over the list of things you have allowed to stop you. Allow your soul to only see those things that are actually relevant to you, and cross out anything that is not.

Getting clear on these lists will do two things.

The first one will give you a sense of what matches with the energy of your true life. It will start you on the pathway to identifying what is congruent and truly matters to you, whilst allowing you to weed out what is no longer relevant anymore.

The second one will help you to identify the blocks or limitations you have made real and true for you that are not. It will also give you an honest sense of what you require to focus on and move beyond in order to truly create a life that you love and that is fun for you.

What we see as blocks are temporary. Many times they are a lie. They may be the things we have made greater than us in order to stop us growing, stop us choosing greater, and distract us from a path that will indeed lead us to what we would like to create.

If the simplicity of this resonates with you and you would like to take this work deeper to truly create a life you love, reach out to me at www.sarahandros.com. You can work with me one-on-one or in a group, and I offer a variety of different programs and trainings tailored to suit you. You can also tune into my new podcast entitled 'The Gift of Being Different'.

I look forward to supporting you to shine, to show up as the greatness of you, and to facilitate you beyond the limitations you have made real or allowed to stop you.

You are a gift. We each are a gift. And until we each see this in ourselves, we may not be able to create the life we came to create. One of my gifts is to look into your soul and SEE you. See what is true. See the YOU beyond all barriers and façades. Is now the time?

Sarah Lee Andros

Sarah Lee Andros

With more than twenty-five years of experience in the healing and wellness industry, Sarah Andros (BA Psychology) is well rehearsed in a multitude of modalities ranging from reflexology and life coaching to the more energetic modalities such as Access Bars® and Symphony of Possibilities®. As an internationally certified Access Consciousness® Facilitator, Sarah is driven to assist her clients to create a life they love, using energetic bodywork alongside coaching for a holistic approach to their health, happiness and well-being.

As a facilitator, Sarah aims to empower people to know what they know, guiding them to a new a sense of possibility within themselves. She has the capacity to see into the depths of a person's being, beyond their walls and barriers, inviting them to show up as the greatest version of themselves. Whether individually or in groups, she instigates massive change in the lives of those she works with and is deeply respected for her capacity to do this. She is also a train-the-trainer, having both inspired and taught many individuals to go on and facilitate consciousness themselves.

This last decade has seen Sarah travel around the globe, allowing her to work with and assist a wide variety of people from different cultures and ways of life. Sarah's main passion is to contribute to creating a more holistic approach to mental wellness in the world.

Websites: www.sarahandros.com & www.accessconsciousness.com/sarahandros
Email: sarah@sarahandros.com
Instagram: sarah_andros
Facebook: Sarah Lee Andros

THE RUNNING WOMAN

Nez Erok

This is my story of a daughter's wound and how I turned my deepest pain into my purpose.

Even from a very young age, I had the belief that I wasn't good enough. This belief spiralled into encompassing every part of my life. I believed that I wasn't thin enough, tall enough, smart enough, pretty enough, worthy enough. I just wasn't enough in any way. Because of the limitations I had placed on myself, my world was distorted to the point where I truly accepted that I was a mistake.

Most of these beliefs stemmed from my relationship with my father. My childhood home was filled with physical and emotional abuse. I never felt safe or in line with my father's expectations, and my first experience with depression came at the age of four.

As I grew up, these feelings of confusion and distrust towards my own father developed into a deep-seated hatred for men. At the age of sixteen, I became lost and suicidal. I was struggling with my studies, and the pressure of going to university and becoming 'somebody and enough' took over.

The voice of my father saying to me 'no matter how many degrees you have, no one will ever love you', rang in my head over and over. I believed him, but I was determined to prove him wrong.

Desperate for my father's love and acceptance, I threw myself into the world of academia and obtained four degrees. But even this level of achievement left me feeling empty inside. I didn't know it yet, but I was seeking 'external validation' through my father's eyes, something that left me feeling empty and lacking.

On the other side of the spectrum was my mother, a woman who lifted me up when my father put me down: balancing the pain with love and tenderness. Seeing how much love she had within her heart and knowing that she, too, was a victim, inspired me as a woman to grow my voice and be heard – a dream of so many women around the world, even in these changing times.

To break out of the moulds and conditioning the world had set out for me, I began discovering and expressing my voice through music. I wrote and performed several songs describing my life experiences and feelings. My most famous song, 'Beautiful', was a raw, emotional and healing song about my childhood. It took me six months to record because every time I went to sing, the song brought up the pain of what I had experienced. I remember crying halfway through so many of the verses as I began healing and discovering the power my voice represented. It allowed me to share this deep wound, to give my inner child a voice that was heard and witnessed, something that she had wanted all those years ago.

After the success of 'Beautiful', which went on to receive awards and recognition from all over the world, I was filled with gratitude. But part of me still felt unfulfilled and unworthy of my success. Like my education, no matter how much I achieved on the outside, I could not connect to my own inner self-esteem and love. This act of external referencing had such a massive impact on how I perceived myself in the world. It wasn't until I looked within and did the internal work that I overcame my pain.

My life and perspective shifted when I was given the book *You*

Can Heal Your Life by Louise Hay and was introduced to the concept of self-love and learnt that doing internal healing work was an act of self-love. Honestly, when I first picked up the book, I thought the author had made an error. What is 'self-love'? My mind couldn't even process such a foreign concept.

Up until this point, I had been conditioned to see myself through a lens of lack and negativity. I hated myself, scolded myself, and never spoke to myself with genuine kindness and gentleness. I was taught that to love yourself was selfish, and I am here to tell you that it is the furthest thing from selfishness.

Reading through the affirmations in the book challenged me. This language was of presence, compassion, understanding. For me, it was a brand-new language.

I love and accept myself.
I forgive myself.
I forgive my father.
I am more than enough.

As an avid learner, I became entranced. I soon became committed to learning this new way of relating to myself, by choosing to unlearn the programming that no longer served me.

Learning to Unlearn

At this point in my life, I was committed to change. I was confident that if I should continue to judge and blame myself for my father's actions and projections, I would never be able to fully live my life. I had a choice. To continue down the same road, which I knew would leave me a lifetime more suffering, or take a risk and climb out of the tiny little box of limiting beliefs that I had trapped myself inside – beliefs that came from a deep-seated wound.

And so I started walking down my new path of neurology, learning that it is possible to change your life by changing your thoughts. You have the power to write a new narrative for yourself; all it takes is a step outside of your comfort zone.

We Can Heal Our Wounds

It is essential to understand that many of us have wounds. It is equally important to know that we can heal our wounds. Each of us has truth beyond our conditions, beyond our scars. No one's wound is less significant or more prominent than someone else's wound. There is a story within each of us, and some of us have wounds that are still bleeding, causing us to suffer whether we are aware of it or not.

In my work as a psychotherapist and life coach, I help my clients unravel their sabotaging belief systems, and I empower them to create a new script based on their choices and new beliefs. In this process, it is essential to recognise that our wounds and their surrounding belief systems do not define us.

I walk my patients through how to un-create the thoughts and belief systems that no longer serve them, as together we focus on how to create new neural pathways based on the beliefs and narratives they create for themselves. I call this new pathway 'life giving versus life taking'. It supports them instead of limiting them.

The Wound is Where the Light Enters You

We have the power and the responsibility to heal our wounds. If we choose not to seek healing, our wounds will fester. They will continue bleeding and creating torment in our lives until we shine a light on the darkness. We can choose to change and heal so that our wounds can become beautifully healed scars: scars that serve as a reminder, as gifts. For me, the gift in my wound was the work that led me to where I am today, helping and healing thousands of people. My beautiful scar is the gift of the wounded healer.

Every Day I Grow

Every day I am constantly learning and growing. I have learnt that we experience self-love by being in acceptance and in allowance of our true selves. From many of my clients, I hear my own story – abusive father, mistrust in men, shame, guilt, lack of confidence and not feeling enough.

I want to take this time and point out the danger in blaming, whether it is your father or someone else, because blaming wounds. In my case, I cannot overlook that my father himself was also damaged. I learnt to forgive my father and accept that he was doing the best he could with what he knew at the time. I had to see my father through eyes of compassion and understanding to see how he became this way. I had to learn about his traumas and see the little boy inside him that was still hurting. I love my father very much, and today we have a healthy, loving relationship.

A New Narrative

In order to heal myself, I had to take my power back from my father. I had to free my inner child from feelings of pain, alienation and entrapment, and I embraced her. I learnt how to love her and give her all of the things she had yearned to get from her father. But this time, it was different. I was in control of the ways I related to myself. I had taught myself a new language, a new narrative of love and appreciation. I had created a new script.

I now teach my clients to do the same, and together we erase the old story that no longer serves them. We decide on a new narrative, one that is *life giving* rather than *life taking*. I help lead my clients down the path that is theirs to take, reminding them of their own divinity – that they are worthy.

At first, this new way in which you perceive yourself almost seems like a lie. It feels risky and foreign because it isn't the way you would naturally relate to yourself. I felt the same way, but continually repeating my affirmations and reminding myself of my new beliefs helped me remember the truth: I am loved, I am beautiful, I am so worthy, I trust myself, I am more than enough, I am plenty!

Choosing Your Belief Systems

I believe that all the events in our lives are ones we attract, ones that have been brought to us by a set of belief systems we hold. What is a belief system? A belief system is simply a collection of thoughts that create a program, narrative or script in our minds. The beautiful thing is that once you change the script, the story changes. How you perceive yourself begins to change the way things manifest on the outside, as if your life is a mirror reflection of your inner world.

In my psychotherapy and life coaching practice, I work with clients on their 'should' list and help them discover their true interests and to live by their values. From there, we can peel back the layers of limiting beliefs that may be in the way of allowing them to live the life they choose. My clients can then begin to design their 'ideal life.' Together, we explore their 'current life' and begin removing those limitations from their present moment.

We only have one life. We are miracles, with a limited time to enjoy and make the most out of this human experience. What I do is all about unravelling the real you through shedding and removing the limitations and masks you've created. Who are you behind the mask that you wear? That is what we'll discover together.

Who is The Running Woman?

The Running Woman is the woman who has not healed. She runs with her many masks and operates from the subconscious conditioning and wounding, not creating from a conscious space. The Running Woman doesn't look into her personal growth because she is afraid of vulnerability, judgment or examining what makes her a certain way. Acting out of fear instead of courage, her boundaries are disowned and distorted.

The Running Woman is imbalanced in her archetypes. She feels like she isn't enough and is unworthy of love – shrinking herself and clipping her wings so that she is unable to soar and take up space. The Running Woman operates from a place of limitation and wounding. The wound that is believed to be right will always confirm itself as truth.

When The Running Woman heals and centres herself on the beauty and truth inherent in her very being, she becomes aware of her power, sovereignty, magic and endless ability to love. I believe we each have the power to heal, learn about ourselves, unlearn the beliefs and sabotaging strategies that shrink us, and intimately know our worth and purpose in this life.

It is my greatest desire to help you stop running. I am here to offer you the support you need to grow and to heal all of those parts of you that need resolution. You are not broken.

Nez Erok

Nez Erok is an award-winning recording artist, counsellor and life coach with extensive professional experience. She is based in Applecross, Perth. She is a member of the Australian Counselling Association (ACA). Nez has a substantial background working in private practice and in the government and non-government sectors.

Nez provides effective therapeutic support and coaching across a diverse range of issues to children, adolescents, adults and couples. Nez's engaging and welcoming approach helps to put her clients at ease and creates a safe space for them to open up and discuss any concerns.

Nez provides unconditional support to her clients, guiding them to achieve insight about their concerns at their own desired pace. In this way, her client's feel heard without judgement and empowered to make changes in their own time and way. Nez is particularly skilled at helping her clients to improve communication, build trust and deepen authentic relationships with self and others.

Nez draws on a range of counselling and coaching approaches, and she responds to individual needs and issues as they arise with a person-centred approach. Some of the therapeutic techniques that Nez uses include: mindfulness-based therapy, solution-orientated therapy, narrative therapy, Gestalt therapy and cognitive behavioural therapy. Nez is committed to help guide her clients to discover ways to live more authentically and at ease within themselves and with others, allowing them to achieve deep personal growth and positive change.

Website: www.zenlifecounselling.com
Instagram: @zenlifecounselling
www.facebook.com/zenlifecounselling
Email: nez@zenlifecounselling.com

BELIEF CHANGE AND ALIGNMENT

Monika Manterys

> Our beliefs control our bodies, our minds, and thus our lives…
>
> – Bruce Lipton

How to overcome self-sabotage and align powerful beliefs to achieve success and fulfilment.

Have you ever felt like you are the victim of circumstances and nothing seems to work in your favour?

Have you ever desired something but inexplicably acted in a way that prevented you from reaching that goal?

Whether your goal is better health, improved relationships, wealth or abundance, belief alignment is the first step to success. If your beliefs are out of line with your purpose, life can feel clunky and difficult.

I want to show you that everything is possible with the right mindset and belief alignment, so you can be inspired and empowered to rise above your self-sabotaging thoughts and behaviours. I want to encourage you to take the next step towards living the life you deeply desire.

My story

I share my story with you because I was once where you might be right now – looking for inspiration, strength and a way to turn your life around.

Though I worked in a mainstream medical profession for twenty years, I had always been interested in natural health and the body's self-healing abilities. I became particularly fascinated in energy medicine and began seeking a science-based approach to explain how energy works inside the human body. One book in particular, *The Biology of Belief* by Bruce Lipton, provided me with enough evidence to put me on a path of exploration, self-discovery and personal growth.

As a cell biologist, Lipton examines the principles of quantum physics, and how it can be integrated into the understanding of how cells process information. He was one of leading scientists who introduced the world to epigenetics, the study of cellular and physiological traits (or external and environmental factors) that switch our genes on and off and define how our cells actually read those genes. Through his experiments and research, Lipton demonstrated that biology follows beliefs.

This inspired me to think deeper, and I was instantly energised because I realised we are neither doomed by our genes nor hardwired to be a certain way for the rest of our lives. I began studying all available material on the mind-body connection and how this relationship significantly influences our health and wellness, and I developed a strong interest in the emerging field of energy medicine.

I started my new training path with Touch for Health Kinesiology, then Kinergetics and the NES Health Bioenergetix wellness system.

These energy healing modalities gave me new understandings and opened my mind to search for more.

I became fascinated with the power of thought, belief and consciousness, and began a journey of personal empowerment and self-discovery. I discovered my own deeply stored childhood traumas, emotional blockages and self-sabotaging beliefs. There were fears and deep-rooted beliefs, such as 'I am not good enough', 'I am not worthy' and 'I don't deserve it'

As I slowly but surely worked through releasing these blocks, the world around me started changing. I realised I am not a victim of my destiny but a powerful co-creator. I can choose the beliefs that will lead me to success and fulfilment. I can build internal belief systems that will serve me well.

I developed an irresistible desire and sense of duty to share what I was learning with others who were looking for hope, direction and change. As a result, in March 2019, I opened my own clinic Mind Body Balance.

What is a belief?

We all have beliefs. Psychology defines them as anything a person currently considers to be true. Beliefs are powerful mental filters that can significantly affect how we see the world and how we behave, feel and communicate. Belief creation starts in early childhood and continues throughout our entire lives. It can be influenced by our environment, other people, experiences, and cultural and social rules.

Our beliefs can be empowering or debilitating, and they can be the difference between failure and success, happiness and unhappiness, and being stuck or thriving. They can nourish or destroy relationships, interfere with or accelerate progress and be the difference between simply existing and living your dreams.

Realising your potential

The French-Burgess Beliefs Gate Model of Human Performance illustrates how our beliefs can either allow us to experience and express our full potential or get in the way of this. The model shows that every person comes into the world with great potential (see the diamond in the illustration) and their belief gates wide open, allowing this potential to flow freely in a newborn baby. However, as life progresses our learning experiences form beliefs that keep the gates open or shut.

Open gates represent positive beliefs that support our success. Conversely, closed gates or partially open gates represent the negative or self-sabotaging beliefs that prevent us from moving towards our desired outcomes. The extent to which a person's potential shines through and positively affects their desired outcomes depends upon how many, and to what extent, belief gates are open or closed.

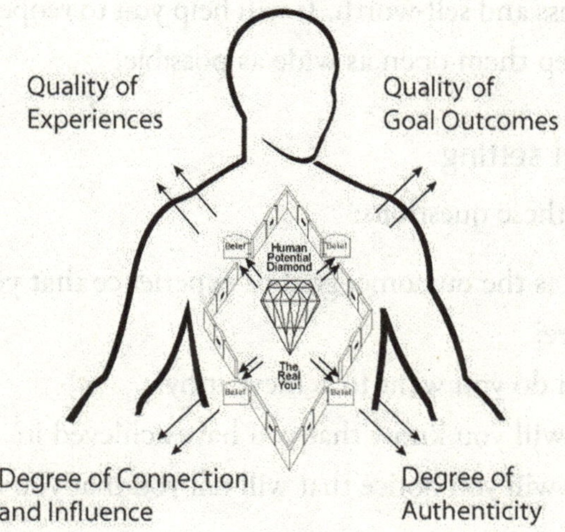

The most positive aspect of this model is that a person's great potential is permanent – the diamond is always shining. If the person is not experiencing this, then it means some belief gates are blocking their shining potential. The good news is that gate closures are only temporary, and any closed gates can be reopened regardless of how long it has been closed.

This model shows that we are powerful creators of our reality. We are free to choose what we want to create and to change the character of our lives by changing our beliefs.

The six-step belief change program

A powerful way for you to overcome self-sabotaging beliefs and to reconnect with your great potential, is the six-step belief change program based on the Belief Gates Personal Empowerment System developed by Tony Burgess and Julie French.

It will help get your beliefs back on track when you embark upon achieving a challenging goal, find yourself in unfamiliar territory or start experiencing doubt and anxiety about your ambitions or resourcefulness and self-worth. It will help you to reopen your 'belief gates' and keep them open as wide as possible.

Step 1: Goal setting

Ask yourself these questions:

- What is the outcome, goal or experience that you want to achieve?
- When do you want to achieve it by?
- How will you know that you have achieved it?
- What will you notice that will tell you that you've achieved it?

- If 10 out of 10 represents achieving your goal and 0 out of 10 is that you haven't yet started, what number best describes where you are in achieving your goal?

Step 2: Belief audit

Say your goal is to run a successful business, but you have a belief that says you are not good with money. This belief is undermining you and creating self-sabotaging behaviours that are stopping you from achieving your goal. Auditing your current helpful and unhelpful beliefs in relation to your desired goals will help you identify sabotaging beliefs that need to change.

- Write as many helpful and unhelpful beliefs that you can in relation to your goal.

Step 3: What if?

Introduce your mind to new possibilities with less self-sabotaging resistance. Stimulate counter positions to current unhelpful beliefs by creating 'what if' questions.

These are examples of 'what if' questions that tend to close our belief gates and get in the way of progress:

- What if all goes horribly wrong?
- What if I'm not good enough?
- What if people think X, Y or Z?

Now ask yourself 'what if' questions that can open belief gates rather than close them:

- What if it is easier than I've been telling myself?
- What if I am more than good enough?
- What if what others think is their business?

Give yourself full permission to counter your unhelpful beliefs, assumptions, thoughts and ideas with as many alternative helpful perspectives as you can. Suspend your judgements about being right or wrong. At this point you do not need to believe new possibilities – you just need to give yourself permission to come up with them.

Remember, the tone of your voice and thinking during this exercise is at least as important as the words themselves. Use a curious and excited tone that will get the attention of your 'inner audience' and inspire curiosity to find out more. This tonality will help to wake up your neuro pathways to new exciting possibilities.

Step 4: Debate

What if … because …

This step is designed to get you arguing with a tonality of conviction for the most helpful possibilities posed by the 'what if' questions. This gives 'legs' to the newly forming helpful beliefs.

- Come up with as many reasons as you can why a statement is true, and debate it like your life depends on it. Use a tone of certainty and conviction to help persuade your inner audience.

For example, rather than saying 'What if I am more capable than I have been telling myself?', remove the 'what if' and instead say 'I am more capable than I have been telling myself because I have successfully achieved many other goals before this one'.

Step 5: Mental rehearsal

Satisfy the part of your brain that likes to learn through experience.

Imagine (using all your senses) experiencing progress and momentum towards your desired outcome, right through to the point where it is achieved and celebrated.

For example, if you argued in step four that 'This will become easier once I get started because I am resourceful and flexible, and I can learn from other people', then imagine progress towards this unfolding easily. Notice how resourceful you are. Notice how flexible you are and how that works for you. Notice how open you are to learning from other people.

Now, imagine having achieved the desired outcome. Look back on your progress, and look ahead to anticipate what comes next. Then reconnect to the present and feel the inspiration. You could also write a passionate, detailed account about experiencing progress and achieving your desired outcome, and then reading it out loud with expression. You could record yourself, and listen to this recording as often as you like. Now your new belief is becoming increasingly authentic and complete.

Step 6: Empowering roles

This step is about modelling your own excellence by stepping into a role that brings the best out of you. This will help confirm your authentic belief change and align with your purpose.

- List all the roles you have been in where people are looking up to you or would look up to you, such as being a parent, teacher/trainer or team leader.
- How can you be the leader you wish you had, who would lead you to the point you want to be?
- Choose your hero. Think of someone you see as a symbol of success and would like to model. Maybe it's someone who already achieved what you desire? Maybe it's someone who, despite obstacles, always rises like a phoenix from the ashes?
- Put yourself into your hero's shoes when you test drive your newly formed beliefs. Or imagine them being with you as you do your best to achieve your desired outcomes

- Ask yourself how your hero would act and what they would say and feel in your situation?
- Your hero is a new version of YOU when you achieve your goal

Keep in mind the words of William Blake: 'Everything that now exists was once imagined.'

Work with me

Contact Monika to guide you through your journey on the six-step belief change programme. She can support you to identify your deeply trapped self-sabotaging beliefs and reopen your belief gates to help you achieve your desired goals and realise your full potential in all areas of your life – better health, business success, improved relationships and more.

By working with Monika, you will begin your journey of resetting your subconscious mind patterns and stepping into living a high-vibrational life that is everyone's birthright.

Monika Manterys

Monika Manterys is the founder of the Mind Body Balance clinic in Wellington, New Zealand. She specialises in BioEnergy scanning/therapies and mindset training. In her clinic she emphasises the importance of the mind–body connection because this relationship has been proven to have significant influence on health and wellness.

She is passionate about helping people find their way back to health and wellness through activating the self-healing abilities of their body. Monika uses NES Health and Healy technologies, along with other techniques, to help her clients identify energy blockages in their mind and body that 'play in a loop' and stop them from living healthy, happy and fulfilling lives.

Monika has a background in nursing, with more than twenty years' experience across a range of clinical and primary care settings. As an independent health researcher, she developed a strong interest in the field of energy medicine. She trained in Touch for Health Kinesiology, Kinergetics, NES Health Bioenergetix wellness system, Energy4Life coaching and the Belief Gates Personal Empowerment System.

Qualifications:

- Belief Change PractitionerNES Health PractitionerEnergy4Life CoachTouch for Health KinesiologyKinergetics
- Bachelor of Education
- Registered Nurse

Special offer:

My special offer for readers of this book is a free NES voice analysis scan with a twenty-minute clarifying call. To access the offer, book 'Free clarifying call' online at: mindbodybalance.co.nz/book-appointment.

Website: mindbodybalance.co.nz
Instagram: instagram.com/manterysmonika
Facebook: facebook.com/mindbodybalancenz
LinkedIn: linkedin.com/in/monika-manterys-017624201

DECODING YOUR MINDSET

Carolyn Sykes

Strength doesn't mean what you're holding isn't heavy. It means it is, and you are holding it.
– Melanie Ann Layer

There are many levels to our mindset. There are also many levels to our being. How we think is just one piece of the puzzle. What drives our thinking is a lot deeper, and how we create positive change is more than just thinking. We need alignment on all levels. Then we are an energetic match for miracles.

It begins with a decision, which comes from the mind. From your decision, your feelings and then your actions follow.

What I have found to be of the most profound benefit is having daily energetic practices to support my new mindsets. These practices are like a daily shower for your mind and energy field. You actually need high amounts of energy (qi) to create and sustain a clear mind. A clear mind is like a high-pressure atmosphere – clear skies filled with sunshine. Low-pressure atmospheres, on the other hand, attract clouds. What I am saying is that, by default, having a clear mind attracts miracles, and that you need to increase your energy to reach that state and to hold it.

Very early on in my twenties, I rode racehorses for a living. I went on the ultimate mindset journey during these years. From seven years of age, I had plenty of experience riding and working with horses. Yet, the first time I sat on one of these epic creatures, I felt a power like none I'd ever felt before. I'd moved away from home and into my digs at a new job. On the first morning I had the most traumatic experience. I couldn't stop the horse. It was the scariest, most out of control feeling I'd ever had. We'd started at the back of the string of about fifteen horses on the gallops that morning. The horse picked up speed, and the more I pulled the reins in a feeble attempt to keep him under control, the stronger and stronger he got. It wasn't meant to be a race, it was just gentle morning exercise. But we started passing all the other horses, and the other riders feared for their safety as I came charging towards them. I managed to stop, eventually. My muscles were shaking and jelly-like. The next day I ached from head to toe. I felt trapped and too scared to go on doing the job, yet I had to. I had no clue about mindset work at the time.

Things came to a head about two weeks in, and my boss sent me to the racing school in Doncaster to learn how to master racehorse riding, where I learnt the proper techniques and, with practice, developed the correct muscles for this very different type of riding. But, my mindset didn't change. I went back to work, waking up terrified every morning, and forced myself through each day. After a time it all got too much and I went back home.

Within the next few years, the most miraculous thing happened. I met my first mentor: a Chinese energy master. They say when the student is ready the teacher appears. I was ready. He taught me about the levels of qi and how to go deep into our psycho-emotional energy system to create a solid foundation for the work of mindset. It is not enough to try to think positive, when the very foundations of your emotional intelligence are shaky.

Fast forward a few years. After spending time on retreat and in one-to-one mentorship, I went back to riding racehorses full-time. I loved it this time around, and I never looked back. I spent another five years loving my career, whilst studying various forms of energy work, meditation and Chinese medicine.

One of the most powerful exercises I learnt was keeping my attention at the point just under the navel. It is called 'keep one point', as you literally keep your attention in this one point. Your mind and body become unified and you become unshakeable. It is instantaneous, and I invite you to try it now.

Work with a partner and ask them to try to push you over. They probably can knock you off balance quite easily. Now try again with all of your attention at one point – five centimetres below your navel. If you can keep your attention there with no thought or distraction, they will not be able to move you. This works in any situation where you need mental or physical strength.

This point, five centimetres below your navel, is your absolute centre. To you, it is the absolute centre of the universe! Keeping your attention here literally centres you. I have taught it often to horse riders, as it helps them immensely with not only their balance for riding, but it also to overcome their feelings of fear and anxiety.

To see a video demonstration of this, head to my website www.theheavensessions.com

You can do this in an instant, the next lesson now is learning to hold it. Anyone can think positive affirmations or be in alignment for a short time, especially when things are going well. The daily practices are where you learn to hold it: hold your attention on one thing for longer and longer periods of time. One of the most obvious daily practices for this is meditation. There are many different types of meditation, just like there are many layers to you. I practice and teach a form of meditation that effortlessly takes you to the awareness of the still, silent presence of NOW. This awareness supersedes thought and is effortless because you do not focus on trying to control thought at all. When you are aware of the presence of now, and can hold your attention on it perpetually, your mind effortlessly mirrors the clear sky.

It is extremely helpful to spend some time daily in this state of no-mind. It develops the muscle of holding your attention one pointedly for longer periods, and it helps you to see through the miasmas of the mind more easily when you are faced with issues as they arise in your life. You can waste a lot of time and energy trying to work out your own mind and trying to force it to be different. For any attempts you make to work long-term, the practices you engage need to be effortless and inherently powerful.

When you identify an issue you want to resolve, it will only work for you if you target the correct level. What does this mean? I'll give you an example. Let's say you have a shoulder issue. Many people go to the doctor, who either prescribes painkillers and exercises, or refers you to a physio. The physio works on your muscles and sends you home with more exercises. This works for some people. It works for some because the issue may have been at the physical level, therefore physical treatment does the trick. What most people aren't aware of is energy, and the connection between all the levels.

Your body speaks your mind. One of the common mind-based causes for shoulder pain can be the chronic thought pattern 'I feel like I've got the weight of the world on my shoulders'. The body manifests the pain to bring attention to the thought pattern that is not serving you. If you don't identify this, then the shoulder does not heal.

Even deeper are our emotions. If you have been feeling sad, which affects the lung organ energetically, your shoulder pain could be a result of the disharmony in the lung meridian channel, which runs through the shoulder. So identifying thought patterns and only working with the mind, in this case wouldn't do the trick either.

We need to take a completely holistic approach to everything. Including mindset. Step one is to make a decision to uplevel in an area of your life. All the other steps combined are the key to making it stick. You need to be strong and fit physically, have good qi and emotional intelligence, as well as an optimistic mindset.

In supporting your mindset it is also important to be well hydrated and take in good nutrition. This is not a nutrition chapter, but when we look at the Hawkins scale of consciousness (below), which ranges from 0-1000, we see that fear calibrates at 100 on the scale. This is an energetic scale, so it is showing you that the energy of fear is at 100. Sugar also vibrates at 100, so if you are eating lots of refined sugars, you will be experiencing a lot of fear. Trying to cover that up with positive affirmations isn't going to work.

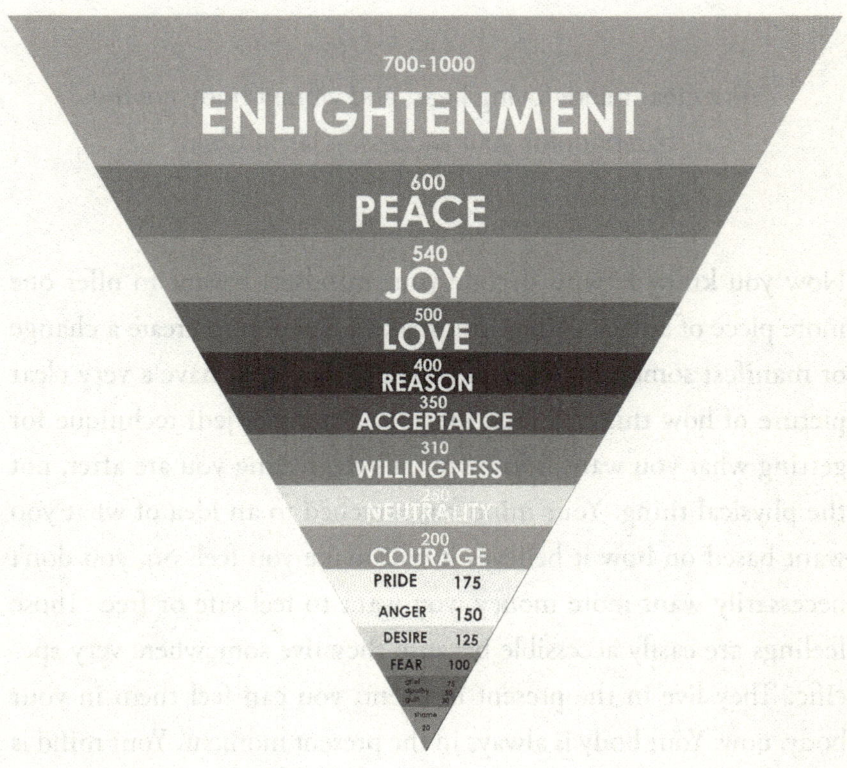

So, if you've been thinking positively and wondering why you haven't been getting the results you were hoping for, I would encourage you to take a look at all the other aspects too.

Take your journal and write in response to the prompts about your diet, exercise, breathwork, energy levels, relationships, and where you feel you are in relation to living your purpose. Getting clear on where you really are in all aspects will really help to decode your mindset. Once you have that clarity, using all of the chapters in this book in conjunction with your mindset work will unlock many more levels for you. The healing journey is infinite and goes deeper and deeper. Blocks may become apparent to you, and new habits in other areas can really support your mindset efforts and create that solid foundation for your clarity of mind to sit upon – like a throne!

> Your clear mind, loving heart and vibrant body are the blueprint for your success. – Jason Chan

Now you know how to decode your mindset, I want to offer one more piece of advice. When you make a decision to create a change or manifest something new in your life, you may have a very clear picture of how this will look for you. The super-jedi technique for getting what you want is knowing it's the feeling you are after, not the physical thing. Your mind has attached to an idea of what you want based on how it believes it will make you feel. So, you don't necessarily want more money, you want to feel safe or free. Those feelings are easily accessible because they live somewhere very specific. They live in the present moment; you can feel them in your body, now. Your body is always in the present moment. Your mind is never in the present moment. If you really take the time to examine the nature of your thoughts, you will see they are all about the past and future. These past and future thoughts create chemical chain reactions in your body, which you feel now – like fear and anxiety. If you want to find the feeling NOW of what you are wanting to manifest in the future, you need to be able to go beyond your mind completely.

This is why I created 'The Heaven Sessions'. The Heaven Sessions are high-level one-to-one coaching sessions, completely tailored to you and designed to help you experience your own version of heaven on earth, now. Not only to experience it energetically, but to help you hold it – hold the vibration of your own heaven, so that you have the feeling now. The manifestation inevitably follows because you are in complete energetic alignment. Allow yourself to imagine for a moment having what it is your heart truly desires; allow yourself to feel the feeling of having it now. You can live from here, and I will show you how.

You can find me at: www.theheavensessions.com.

Carolyn Anne Sykes

Carolyn is a licensed acupuncturist and meditation coach. She has run a busy clinical practice for the last seven years and has also taught meditation to individuals and companies. She has organised and hosted events for leaders in the industry, and is proud to have been personally mentored by the late Barefoot Doctor (Stephen Russell), Jason Chan and Ishaya monk, Sandy Newbigging.

Carolyn helps people from all walks of life to increase their life-force energy, which allows their bodies to heal and their minds to settle into present moment awareness. The ultimate goal of her work is to assist you to achieve Inner Peace.

Carolyn is so passionate about what she does because she feels incredibly blessed to have been gifted with her mentors so early on in her life and career. Nothing makes her happier than sharing these transmissions of wisdom.

Carolyn is currently enjoying spending as much quality time as possible with her beautiful nine-month-old baby boy, whilst simultaneously offering The Heaven Sessions – transformative one-to-one life coaching.

Website: www.theheavensessions.com
Facebook: Carolyn Sykes Lic Ac

DECODE ENERGY MASTERY

INTRODUCTION

Tracey Jewel

Be the energy you want to attract.

I've known for a long time that everything is connected by energy. I've been super sensitive and felt the energy of others and taken it on as my own. I've also allowed my energy to get the better of me or to permeate others.When I came across the quote by Nikola Tesla 'If you want to find the secrets of the universe, think in terms of energy, frequency and vibration', it resonated with me immediately. At the same time I also came across the frequency device Healy in late 2019. It was the missing energetic piece to my Wellness practices! (More about the Healy later!)You see, high vibe energy is about becoming aligned with your highest, most authentic self, which allows you to show up as your absolute best. When you're in alignment with your truth, you raise your energetic vibration (bring on the good vibes). In the next few chapters, we can help you connect to your truth so you can feel more joyful, energised, and inspired. Remember, your energy is your greatest source of power.

While some people may think that unlocking this energetic potential and embarking on a spiritual awakening equates to instant bliss, this isn't exactly the case. Waking up to a new level of consciousness requires you to live and see the world in a brand-new way. It's not for the faint-hearted. You go about your work, building your business, raising your family, all while seeing the deep division between light and dark in the world and within yourself.

This is why so many find themselves in familiar places, lulled into complacency and old patterns. Even while part of them still longs for profound, lasting transformation found in the form of more freedom, happiness, harmony, financial success, satisfying relationships, and a sense of profound peace and fulfillment that comes from being aligned with their purpose.

Real seekers try and try again, always looking for the next step, unknowingly addicted to the spiritual highs and suffering the lows that await them on the other side.

An Endless Chase

For these people, all of the knowledge they've gained is somehow unable to create the lasting change they've been looking for. Why? There's a good reason for this. Let's break it down.

Knowledge is power, but only if you have the right information. Some information, while interesting, may do little to benefit you on your current journey. And other information is just flat-out wrong (Law of Attraction teachings, anyone?).

Even the valuable and relevant information you do have may be a mishmash of tools and spiritual practices without a grounding, natural system in place. Without a system—a proven, step-by-step process to keep yourself aligned with your highest spiritual goals – there is no way to get consistent results.

It's You

So you're right: something *is* holding you back and derailing your progress. But it's not the Universe, it's not other people, it's not bad luck—It's you.

Or rather, it's your old patterns and programs that have boxed you into a specific set of experiences, like a happiness thermostat that's constantly set at 'OK' or 'Fine.' When you start to move outside of that little zone, your familiar programming switches on and brings you back into 'reality.'

What will it take to move you beyond these limitations and into the transcendental? A system. But not just any system: one that teaches you to clear old, stagnant energy and release the deep-rooted beliefs and psychological programming that hold you back.

This system has helped those individuals solve issues such as:

- chronic migraines and fatigue
- severe illness and disease
- anxiety, depression, addiction
- deep-rooted traumas and inner conflict
- troubles in relationships (without compromising values)
- business failures turned around in record time.

In the following chapters, you'll get to learn many of these systems and start to implement them into a high frequency lifestyle and experiences.

HOW TO RAISE YOUR OWN VIBRATION

Amy Bingham

I have lived a life of many challenges. Heck, we all have, that's our process for growth, right? How do you know if you are really processing your challenges in a way that allows for your most divine growth? Do you know how to take every situation, thought and event and navigate it free from judgement, from self-sabotage, from limiting beliefs, energetic blocks, and conditions that no longer serve you? How does one get to this place?

Many people are launched into a spiritual awakening after great loss (job loss, loss of dreams, death, trauma, and so on) specifically because the experience shakes them to the core to move into higher level of consciousness.

I've been to the depths of grief with many losses. One particularly difficult year, I experienced a handful of miscarriages, the unexpected and traumatic death of my seventeen-year-old son while six months pregnant, giving birth just three months after that immense loss, then having to go through a divorce. I spent a long time navigating life in survival mode as a grieving mother, now left to raise an infant and toddler. I honestly didn't think I could ever regain hope and be a mother again, after losing my soulmate – my firstborn son.

I tried to find strength in every beautiful grief quote, but they all said that I'll just learn to live 'with' my grief, and it will now become my new normal. I found myself years later still letting my truth be that I would grieve forever, and that there was no end in sight for this pain. I tried to be present with my little kids, but I found myself being pulled between two worlds: the world my angel son constantly pulled me into, to walk down memory lane with him, and this world where I had little children that needed to be cared for.

I remained deep in survival mode, not functioning, for over 1000 days. Over 1000 days of continually, ruthlessly operating from a 'no will to live' state of mind. I was about to lose my career, a career I had dedicated the last fifteen years to and had worked so hard on creating, and I was ready to give up on life.

But then, one day, I said out loud with such force: 'grief no longer works for me'. I realised it was not serving me in any way – not living, loving or breathing. I couldn't imagine doing another single day of grief, let alone another forty years of it. In that moment I chose to no longer live with grief. Finally, I surrendered to Source/God/the pure beings of Unconditional Love and asked them to take everything: to strip me away from everything that I was made from, to allow me to start from a pure place of being. I offered to give up my home, job, security, family, whatever it took for them to just show me a different way to be living. It was in this process of surrender that I learnt things it would have otherwise taken me hundreds of years to understand.

I was shown that a magical world exists on the other side of surrender. That if we all completely and wholeheartedly just let go, we will be rebirthed and shown how our soul was meant to be dancing in this life. It is our birthright to live a vibrant, full and abundant life, yet we quickly forget this throughout our journey.

Now I knew I could completely rewrite the rest of my life path and release the trauma I had kept such a strong grip on because I felt grief was the last remaining tie to my son. I got to rewrite my truth about living the most full, vibrant and abundant life after grief. Here's where the beautiful sacred process of a divine rebirth unfolds. Where I learnt how to raise my own vibration.

Are we really ready to be freed from our traumas, grief, heartbreak, disappointments, could haves and should haves? Some will never think it's possible to reach this kind of freedom. Luckily you get to claim what works for you and what does not serve you. So this is where I ask you to sit in the depths of every emotion and cry from every single cell in your body that had your trauma imprinted on it. And then ask what needs to be released. Ask what you are holding onto that is not allowing your soul to be aligned with the highest vibration level that you are meant to be living from. And then ask your higher self to release everything that is no longer serving you and allow healing. Surrender to this letting go process. The moment you bring awareness to what needs to be released, it surfaces to allow you to do the work on it. This is how we constantly raise our vibration.

> Maybe the journey isn't so much about becoming anything. Maybe it's about un-becoming everything that isn't really you, so you can be who you were meant to be in the first place. — Paul Coelho.

We naturally vibrate at a very high frequency, but we've picked up many things through our experiences that have lowered our vibration. We just need to release – release all the pain, the limiting beliefs about ourselves, about who we really are as divine beings.

Take a moment and write down what really is buried deep inside you that truly needs to be released. Maybe it's something small that doesn't surface very often, yet you know it is holding you back from true inner peace. And then journal for the next few days about what has come up now that you have allowed awareness into the pieces you need to 'un-become'. Then you will start noticing repeating thought patterns, unnecessary fear or negative behaviours that are not for your highest good. And when these appear, repeat: 'I am open to healing, I am open to releasing, I am open to receiving'. Breathe slow and deep every time you need to repeat this release mantra, and you will start to notice shifts. To heal ourselves, we have to bring the part of us that needs healing to our awareness.

As I sit and think about all the ways our souls can ascend and how we can raise our vibration to higher and higher levels of consciousness, one thing to know is that we all have the same amount of ability to do this. We all have the same ability to heal ourselves, to raise our vibration and reach the same growth, by design. We are all made for this kind of work. We all have the choice to awaken to our own divine rebirth: to reinvent, rebuild, recreate, redesign our lives over and over again, as many times as our soul desires to be rebirthed into new light, into a higher vibration.

The biggest question is, how bad do you want it? You say you want a new way of living and breathing, and accepting abundance, adventure and love. But, if I told you a rebirth is required, that you need to give up the attachment to your old identity and start completely over, would you still want it? If I told you that you are divinely guided and divinely supported, would you surrender at that point?

Every person who has reached higher levels of consciousness holds this truth of being divinely guided and supported, and they want you to know this truth deep in your soul as well. All you have to do is surrender, so that everything can shift. And every time you surrender, call in your higher self and your divine beings of light to support you while you let go of everything and lean into the unknown. It is here, in the unknown, where you get to play in higher consciousness, bringing new thoughts, new patterns, new healing, new ways of living – all raising your vibration into higher consciousness. You can't achieve this if you are operating from a place of expected outcome, fear, forced and rigid energy. Let go hon, just let go, and trust you are divinely guided and protected.

When I do energy healing on my clients, I always connect them to their higher self. We are always connected to our guides, our higher self, God, and divine source, but I re-introduce the connection for those who have forgotten. I show my clients how to feel their spirit team presence and start communicating with them as their guide, so they can start walking with this support and tap into their own intuition. And it's in these moments where rebirth happens, where you are launched into a spiritual awakening of no return. And the more you surrender to the unknown and trust your intuition, the higher and higher you vibrate and reach divine consciousness.

Raising your vibration to the highest level of consciousness isn't for the weak. So are you really committed to your soul's growth?

We get to release the stories we have been telling ourselves. Stories of unworthiness, stories of self-shaming. We also get to rewrite the endings of these stories. We can change a story of 'he left me, people always leave me, why am I hard to love'. This thought pattern shuts off our heart energy to protect ourselves, while at the same time feeding us unkind thoughts. Instead, we can feed our heart energy with love and acceptance. In this example, you can change your thoughts to: 'Thank you for giving me an opportunity to see where I have been lacking self-love, and thank you for removing the connection so I can now heal and grow from this experience.' Now you have rewritten this ending and wrapped it with self-love. Our entire experience is driven for and by our soul, to enable us to achieve higher consciousness, greater self-love and raise our own vibration. So shift the stories you write about experiences that have come to an end. Wrap each one up in self-love, wrap them up with an awareness and growth mindset. If everything happens for us, not to us, how does that shift your mindset and the stories you've told yourself?

Take a moment to write down a story you'd like to rewrite the ending of. If you could write the ending to be the most beautiful story for your own growth – free of judgement and from judgement of others, free of shaming and disappointment for yourself – how free do you think you would be to change your narrative? If you skip this step in an ending, the step where you give gratitude for the opportunities, awareness, healing and growth it gave you, you won't truly be breaking free from any pain, patterns, habits or what you had attracted into your energy field. Flood the experience with pure love, so you can start your next adventure with your new mindset, new strength, new self-love and step into your new soul power.

This is how you can raise your own vibration, by finding divine purpose in every situation.

I knew what the depths of child loss felt like – it was pure hell. Now I was ready to live, breathe and bathe in the vibration of Pure Inner Peace. I needed to rewrite the ending of the physical journey for me and my son. My soul ached to understand what inner peace felt like. When you ask your higher self what you are holding onto that needs to be released, it is in these moments that you will understand the opposing feeling, that you are seeking to help raise your vibration.

While you are doing this work to heal, release and raise your own vibration, it's imperative to understand how to protect your energy from external influences.

You form life force energetic cords with people you interact with, and you form these cords all throughout the day. Let's say you spoke in person with someone today. Energetic cords were formed between you and this person. That person then leaves and has thoughts about you, about their understanding of you, about whether they think your thoughts or actions are right or wrong according to their beliefs, about how capable you are – thinking from their own fears and limitations. All these thoughts are now in the energetic cords that were formed from your connection. And that energy could be conflicting with what you are creating, with how you are trying to heal, with what you are manifesting. If you seem stuck in your growth, make sure you don't have energetic cords with energy that is conflicting with your journey. We pick these up all throughout the day, without even knowing it. To keep your energy protected as you raise your vibration, find a good clearing mantra.

Over the next week, every night as you end your day repeat this is prayer/mantra:

> I lovingly release any energetic cords I may have picked up or formed myself throughout the day that do not belong to my journey, that are not serving my highest good, that are bringing in lower energy vibrations, that are disrupting my life path. I replace this energy with pure divine unconditional love.

If you have a hard time connecting with what it is that needs to be released for you to be operating from your pure energy, try this inner child exercise.

Picture yourself at a very young age. Pull in details of your age, hairstyle, clothes, environment if needed, to truly connect to this younger version of yourself. Picture your inner child entering the room and sitting down on the floor in front of you. You walk up to her and sit down next to her. You both glance into each other's eyes and smile with love. Now ask your inner child what she needs. Ask her what she can now tell you that you couldn't ever hear before. Your inner child will always tell you something you need to let go of or that you need to embrace. Can you hear her?

Now, do you have an idea of what your inner child has been lacking? Maybe it's more playfulness and less stress, maybe it's self-love and acceptance, safety and protection, nurturance or understanding. And it's here, in this moment of self-reflection, that you realise you are the provider of these needs for yourself.

What is the feeling you would like to bring in that you are lacking? Once you lock into a feeling, the universe matches the vibration of that feeling. If the feeling is operating from fear, it is a lower vibration. If it is coming from pure love, it is a higher vibration. We raise our vibration by specifically feeling into the emotion that we want to match. This can be done through meditation, 'I am' affirmations, connecting to your soul through sacred dance, daydreaming of magic unfolding, and feeling, I mean really feeling, what that is like. Find every way to have a tiny experience of that feeling each day. If you are seeking more playfulness, and magical and sensual feelings of joy, put a post-it note on your tea cabinet that says 'which flavour of tea do I want to be pleasured with today?'. And then, when you sip your tea, sit consciously and feel into all the sensations of the flavours.

I was seeking inner peace. This was the opposing feeling to where grief resided for me. Meditation was the key for me to connect back to my soul and find inner peace. And strengthening my intuition and connection to my higher self were the keys for me to reach higher vibrations of consciousness and inner peace. Once you find the feeling you want the universe to match you with, sit in the magical experience of that feeling for as long as you can, and keep inviting this energy in every day. You will be subconsciously and consciously attracting it to appear in all aspects of your life.

Raising your own vibration is about letting go of everything that doesn't serve you, as your true soul essence is of the highest vibration. As you let go, you are creating a new rebirth for your soul. We are in the rebirth era of our time. This is a choice that we are all entitled to. The energy is here. The power that we are is now alive. This the rebirth of our time. You came here specifically for this. We came to rise, we came to be the calm, we came to be the oceans wave, the stars in the dark sky. It is rebirth time!

We are all here to live a vibrant life, and we are all worthy of it. What does your rebirth look like? How will you step into your rebirth, redesigning your entire new life path?

You get to choose your rebirth, and in this moment you are new again! All you need to do is:

Quiet Your Mind

... Quiet Your Space

... ... And Lean Into Your Glow

Amy Bingham

Amy Bingham is the owner of Lean Into Your Glow. A project that has blossomed into a life changing experience. Amy primarily spends her time as a motivational speaker, an energy healer, a spiritual transformational mentor and author – sharing her real and raw depth of trauma and awakening.

Amy spent years navigating life as a single mum, working hard to build her career in the information technology industry. She's been to the depths of grief with many losses: one year, in particular, experiencing, while six months pregnant, the unexpected and traumatic death of her seventeen-year-old son, giving birth just three months after that immense loss and getting a divorce.

She found a way to surrender and honour the grief experience she was thrown into. The soul journey for her was to feel every real and authentically raw emotion of her grief: emotionally and mentally healing herself and others along the way through her process of self-discovery, self-love and self-healing.

Amy empowers others into their soul rebirth, returning to their higher-self, bringing them back to remembrance of the way their soul was always meant to be living.

Website: LeantIntoYourGlow.com
Facebook: https://www.facebook.com/amy.bingham.11
Instagram: abingsassy

CONNECTION WITH YOUR HORMONES AND CYCLES

Stacey Foat

The only limitation to what you can create in your life, is the limitation of your imagination.

– Stacey Foat

Hating on our hormones

It has become a toxic culture of blame. We point the finger at our hormones for every little thing that goes wrong in our lives, from uncomfortable physical symptoms right through to those irrational emotional outbursts we project on others. The truth is, it's not our hormones per se, rather it's the disconnection we feel from our physical bodies and the resulting inability to recognise the messages our hormones are trying to send to us.

It is this disconnection that has women suffering, feeling more confused than ever, struggling with the symptoms of hormonal imbalance: mood swings, acne, weight gain. As well, there has been an astronomical increase in reproductive disorders, such as endometriosis, PCOS and infertility.

We're so busy in a world that we cannot keep up with, that we don't have the time to stop and listen to our bodies anymore. Our first response is to take a hormone pill to suppress our symptoms, but in doing so we silence our body's only way of telling us what it needs.

Far too many women have developed a hate for their menstrual cycle, dreading that ghastly time of the month, naively using birth control pills to 'skip' their bleed because, sadly, each cycle has become a physically and emotionally excruciating occurrence.

So how can we take back control of our bodies and learn the language of our hormones?

Your menstrual cycle and your hormones are your superpower!

Although it is common, with one in eight women believed to be suffering from what the wider public would perceive as a hormone imbalance, it is certainly not normal to experience pain and discomfort with your menstrual bleed, or skin breakouts and emotional breakdowns for that matter. These signs and many other symptoms are your body's way of letting you know that you are physically, emotionally and spiritually out of balance or, in other words, completely disconnected from the innate wisdom you possess within you. The body communicates through sensation, and the fastest way to get your attention is through pain and discomfort. Are you listening?

Hormones are chemical messengers. The delicate ebb and flow of oestrogen and progesterone, that changes throughout the monthly cycle, is a gift, with its power largely untapped by most women. What we possess is an internal navigation system, which, when understood and correctly utilised, is a beautiful tool for helping us to truly experience life through the emotions that influence our vibration, the energy source from which we create! Embodiment, or the 'feeling' of emotions, is how we tune into our intuition. It's how we learn who we are, our values and our beliefs, and it completely shapes the way we perceive the world around us and, ultimately, what events, people and magic or drama we attract into our lives.

Our hormones give rise to changes in neurotransmitters. They are the reason we feel. They are an inbuilt GPS that directs us away from danger and unpleasant experiences (or people) and towards experiences that elicit joy, love, health and abundance. Our hormones are the reason we get to experience the creative fire of our womb that fuels our passions and drives us to create everything that shows up in our world. Without hormones behaving out of balance and steering us away from detrimental choices, we wouldn't have the internal navigation to lead us to the love and excitement that arises from following our true purpose.

When we start to live our life out of alignment, engaging in too much risky, toxic behaviour and making lifestyle choices that are out of touch with our values and dreams, our hormones will fall out of balance and our menstrual cycles will go out of whack. This is a gift from your higher self, warning you that you are off your life path and the path you are on is not going to create the fulfillment you, as a human soul, desires.

Hormone hell to hormone harmony

At age twenty-seven, I was in my social prime, playing hard and living large. I was fresh out of university, working full-time and studying yet another online course, as my need to add more qualifications to my name was obsessively motivated by an underlying lack of self-belief and a feeling that I would never be 'enough'. I was exercising like a beast, because ever since I could remember I'd hated my physical body, and because pounding the pavement seemed like the perfect punishment for the fact I couldn't control my sweet tooth. On top of all this I was a professional socialite suffering from a severe case of 'fear of missing out', so partying was just like my other full-time job. I was having the time of my life so, as you can imagine, it was a major inconvenience when my health came crashing down. Before I knew it, I'd hit adrenal fatigue. I was weighing a solid ten kilograms heavier than what was healthy for my frame, I had broken out in cystic acne, I was chronically exhausted, and I had been awarded the exciting diagnosis of polycystic ovarian syndrome with a side of premature ovarian failure or, as one endocrinologist believed, I had entered menopause – age twenty-seven.

But, the thing I must point out is that this mess didn't just happen overnight. My body and my hormones had been giving me warning signs for many years, but I refused to listen because I was a 'go getter' and I strongly believed if you wanted to 'get' anywhere in life you had to work hard and stay busy. So, with my heavy training, studying, working and social schedules, I was what you could say, burning the candle at both ends and completely ignoring my body's cries for help.

Stop shooting the messenger!

By definition hormones are chemical messengers. Their job is to send signals and information from organ to organ in order to catalyse the necessary changes required to carry out the physiological functions which keep us alive.

Your hormones are not the bad guys, they are not the reason you are exhausted and emotional. In fact, your hormones have nothing to do with it. They are just the ones relaying the message. The real question is, what triggered the change in the 'normal' hormone levels to make them imbalanced? Remember, your hormones are just responding to your body's immediate internal and external environment and its physiological needs.

A hormone imbalance itself is not a disease. It is merely the result of your overall health: the toxic load within your cells, your nutritional status, stress levels, hydration, infections, gut microbiome and, of course, your spiritual and emotional health – how much you are loving yourself, following your passions and living your truth!

When we stop blindly blaming our hormones and actually investigate what your 'imbalanced hormones' represent, not only will the hormone related symptoms disappear, but our hormones will have no reason to 'behave badly' any longer.

Living in alignment from a place of truth and authenticity

They say we all have a purpose, a reason to be here. Our soul enters this world on a mission, and the aim of the game of life is to find yours and live it! There's so much we can set out to achieve – goals we can create and plans we can make – but at the end of the day, the most important thing in life is living your truth based on your key values and what makes you happy.

Your values are the basic, fundamental beliefs that act as your moral compass and influence your everyday choices and attitude to situations, ultimately shaping your personality. When we start to stray from our core values and make decisions that don't align with our truth, our energy becomes weaker and the signs of stress will begin to show in our health, especially through classic hormone related symptoms. Living in alignment is truly knowing yourself, your values, emotional needs, desires, hobbies, priorities and your greatest dreams for this lifetime. These are the things that make up our 'purpose'.

From a space of inner knowing, we are able to speak our truth with an open heart and from a place of love, without projecting judgement upon others with differing opinions. We have the courage and vitality to chase our dreams because we are so closely connected to the feelings associated with achieving the things that mean the most to us.

But, most importantly, having a strong sense of who you are allows for clear boundaries and identifies what we will and won't tolerate from other people or situations. This knowing allows for self-love and self-respect and keeps us closely connected with our intuition and more open to recognising the subtle messages from our body and higher self.

When you are experiencing disease of any nature, this is generally a sign you have become disconnected from your truth. Living in alignment involves a commitment to doing the inner work, taking the time to sit with yourself and learn about who you are and what lights you up. Feeding your soul requires that you invest time and energy into creating fun, healthy and intellectual endeavours that expand your conscious awareness and fill your heart and soul with joy. It's having curiosity to explore the world in order to discover what ways of living align with your values and your dreams.

Vibration is everything

Your vibration is like your inner light. How brightly you shine is ultimately determined by your beliefs, which shape how you perceive everything you encounter. This then directly influences what emotional response you will have to life's events. From an outside perspective, your vibration and how much you glow is kind of like your unspoken world, a frequency you are emitting, which is how the rest of the world sees you.

Although, many of us would like to believe that it's our

'imbalanced' hormones that influence our mood, thoughts, feelings and attitude to life, it is actually the opposite. Your vibration has a direct impact on your health and hormones, which comes back to your beliefs. These govern the thoughts you have and the choices you make.

The problem is, 90 per cent of our thoughts are unconscious, which means we're not even aware we are having them until a situation arises that triggers an emotional response if the situation contradicts a belief we hold and live by. Being triggered into an uncomfortable emotional response, although often confronting at the time, is an amazing opportunity to re-evaluate our beliefs and reassess whether they are allowing us to live in alignment with our goals and purpose in life. Sometimes we need to change our perception of a situation in order to see it more clearly, allow for the growth and evolution of our soul or bring about a different, more successful outcome in our life in regards to our healing journey, relationship choices or career, and so forth.

Our beliefs are formed from the things we are exposed to in our childhood, conditioned by society and largely influenced by our family, friends and peers. Ultimately, our environment largely forms our beliefs, and as a result determines our personality, a key player in what we experience in life.

No one consciously chooses to feel triggered or willingly creates dis-ease in their physical body, but whether we are aware of it or not, what we create is a consequence of our beliefs and our perception of events, and all this is driven by our subconscious beliefs and emotional blueprint.

The same applies to our hormones. When we are consistently choosing 'shitty' thoughts and living from a place of fear and judgement, we are polluting our body with toxic, acidic, inflammatory and low vibrational energies that hurt the body, physically, emotionally and spiritually.

Emotional Evolution

This is the process of identifying limiting beliefs that are keeping us disconnected from what we desire in life.

Awareness, Acceptance, Alignment

There are three stages of emotional evolution that allow us to work through our triggers or 'dis-eases' of the body in order to identify the core belief that is negatively polluting our vibration and affecting our ability to resonate the frequencies of love, happiness, expansion, health and abundance.

Step 1 – Awareness

How can we take charge of our vibration if we have all these limiting beliefs lurking around in our subconscious that we aren't even aware of?

Awareness is the identification of these limiting beliefs, the ones that keep up from our truth and keep us separate from achieving all that we desire. For the most part, conscious awareness is generally only found when we don't get what we want. More often than not we are well aware of what we don't want, but we can be confused about what we do want. When something goes wrong or we are triggered, awareness of what we want instead can be formed. Sometimes things have to fall apart before we can truly recognise what it is we want.

And although circumstances like these can be extremely painful and disappointing as they unfold, there is always wisdom and growth to be found if we can surrender to the fact that everything happens for a reason.

When you are triggered, self-inquiry is one of the most powerful tools you can utilise – the process of exploring, at a deeper level, exactly what has transpired and what it means to you.

Awareness requires identifying the story your ego has attached to the events that have unfolded. Here you are able to identify the limiting belief that has been controlling your emotional blueprint, silently hijacking your vibration and largely influencing the events that occur in your day-to-day life.

Step 2 – Acceptance

Acceptance is principally about surrendering, being willing to let go of what you thought you knew as true, and broadening your perspective as a way of redirecting you back to your truth. Life happens for us, not to us. Every event is an opportunity to re-evaluate, transform our beliefs and shift our vibration back to love.

This involves the art of not reacting to our triggers and, instead, pausing and reconnecting with our breath, which allows a more subjective look at the situation. From this place we are more likely to recognise that this 'hiccup' has happened for our greater good, and that we can move through it and come out stronger and more positive on the other side if we are willing to learn from it. At this stage of emotional evolution there must be an acceptance that this has occurred for a reason, as a catalyst to change your beliefs and therefore change your reality.

When we are willing to surrender and change our beliefs, we

are quite often able to set ourselves free from a lot of unnecessary internal suffering.

Step 3 – Alignment

As we have learnt, alignment is about living in our truth, the space where our vibration matches the frequency of joy and love. From this energy we are most powerful in our ability to create or, as some would say, manifest. We create our reality through our thoughts, which are governed by the beliefs that shape our perception. Living in alignment is taking action on a daily basis to ensure your thoughts and choices are aligned with all that you desire.

Emotional evolution in action

Let's say that you have been suffering with a debilitating, hormone related condition such as endometriosis. The emotional counterpart of that disease process is the limiting beliefs that have associated with them suppressed anger and self-shaming, which you were not consciously aware of as those emotions remained buried deep within your uterus, creating the stress and disease at a cellular physical level. The emotions are not brought into conscious awareness until an event occurs that triggers their release. In this case, an anger outburst provides you with an opportunity to explore why the situation has angered you so much and what the associated limiting belief is that is creating a weakened, low frequency vibration that is more receptive to disease. After a period of self-inquiry, the acceptance will take place if you are open to shifting your perspective, and from there aligned action can be taken to move you to a vibration of love, forgiveness and joy.

The key to alignment is tapping into your inner child and connecting with your imagination. We can create anything we can visualise and feel. Create a new story and align your life to this new belief, adopting new habits and making changes in your day-to-day life that allow you to stay in the high vibrating frequency of your new empowered belief that is more aligned to love and self-acceptance.

The only limitation to what you can create in your life is the limitation of your imagination. We must teach ourselves how to feel a certain way and fantasise this new reality before we can bring it into existence, by wiring our brain and our thoughts and changing our frequency so that we are the vibrational match to that which we desire. Feel it. Create it.

If you are keen to learn more about creating your reality and the process of emotional evolution, check out Stacey's book, *Trigger Happy*, a guide to inner work and creating the life of your dreams.

Emotional Evolution is an online interactive program that teaches you the exact steps and skills to working through triggers and understanding the emotional language of the body and how it relates to disease so that you can align yourself to true health, love, abundance and emotional freedom.

Stacey Foat

A degree qualified naturopath and nutritionist, Stacey is dedicated to a truly holistic approach to wellness by encompassing physical, emotional and spiritual elements, empowering and educating women to take charge of their healing journey, through body awareness and the understanding of their natural hormonal cycles.Stacey utilises the Emotional Evolution™ process, which identifies limiting beliefs and blockages to healing, reconnecting women to their full creative potential and ability to heal.In recognising our hormones are merely messengers and that our body's symptoms are a cry for help, Stacey identifies the true underlying imbalances and unmet needs of the individual and helps them to reconnect with their feminine energy so that they can lead a truly fulfilling, energised and limitless life!'I fell into this area of expertise, after being told at the age of twenty-seven that I had commenced menopause.' Having struggled with PCOS for many years, I soon realised that the conventional approach to treating hormone related conditions by silencing the symptoms with synthetic hormone birth control pills was never going to work and was only digging myself into a deeper hole. This was where the Balanced Babes signature 7 Step Hormone healing system was created, as these were the exact steps taken to not only reverse my premature ovarian failure, clear up the cystic acne and lose the PCOS related weight gain but, most importantly, to enable me to naturally conceive my daughter, something I was told by mainstream doctors would never be possible.'I'm currently working on the launch of my latest online program, Emotional Evolution, and the accompanying book, *Trigger Happy*, which are a guide to inner work and addressing the spiritual and emotional elements of your healing journey.'

Website: www.balancedbabes.com.au
Instagram: https://www.instagram.com/staceyfoat_balancedbabes/
Facebook: https://www.facebook.com/groups/balancedbabes4life/

HOW TO PROGRAM YOUR UNCONSCIOUS MIND FOR SUCCESS

Leanne Kerrison

Gratitude opens the door to … the power, the wisdom, the creativity of the universe. You open the door through gratitude.

Programming the unconscious mind for a happy, productive life is something I am very passionate about. My wish for you is to really understand how easy it is to program your unconscious mind for more happiness and success.

How incredibly empowering it is to train your brain in this way. You can change limiting beliefs and unconscious patterns of thought and behaviour that may be outdated and not working for you anymore.

Your unconscious mind can easily be programmed to achieve the results you desire in your life. Creating new neural pathways in your mind is the secret to your success.

You will discover how you can influence and change the thought patterns of your mind, to be more positive, calm, productive and happy, allowing you to achieve the results you want your life.

Scientists have already proven that your brain is being changed, shaped and moulded with life experiences every day. Your brain is literally being shaped and influenced with the events of your life, past and present. This very exciting scientific breakthrough has significantly amplified our understanding of how we can increase our happiness, improve our health and change habits – and even change our genetics. This is called neuroplasticity.

Neuroplasticity is the study of the plastic and malleable nature of our brains and the basis for the possibility of transforming our minds. By practising new ways of thinking and mobilising our thoughts, we can rewire and reshape the way our brains work. This then can increase our happiness levels.

I have worked with clinical hypnotherapy for many years. In my clinic, Advanced Clinical Hypnotherapy, I have helped many people reduce stress, increase happiness and achieve the success they desire.

I have helped many people rewire their minds/brains for success, and I have witnessed so many wonderful transformations in mind and body when the unconscious mind is open and ready to receive new learnings.

Programming the unconscious mind for success can be achieved easily, effortlessly and naturally, utilising and harnessing the power of your own mind with hypnosis.

What is the unconscious mind?

Psychology explains, the subconscious mind is the part of your mind that is not in your current awareness. It is like a huge memory bank that stores your beliefs, your memories, your skills and your previous experiences. This part of the mind also operates via your autonomic nervous system, which keeps your heart beating, your lymph system working, your digestion working and your eyes blinking, without you being consciously aware.

Your unconscious mind can hold information that is outside of your conscious awareness. This can be described as your blueprint, your programming.

The 'blueprint' of your belief systems can be imprinted from birth, even before birth, in utero and up to the first seven years of your life, all in the unconscious mind.

Your map of the world can depend on how you were raised as a child, the environment in the home where you grew up and in your experiences in life. These blueprints or programs can be generational and/or outdated, and can sabotage your motivation, productivity and happiness.

Have you ever wondered how people can have different emotional reactions to the same situations in life? Everybody thinks, feels and hears the world differently, all based on their own experiences.

Most people are operating on old, outdated thought programs, maybe programs they were taught, heard or were wired in as children. Some of these outdated thought programs can be statements like 'You cannot leave the table until you eat everything on your plate', 'You're not good enough', 'You're not pretty enough' or 'You're not clever enough'.

These blueprints or programs in your unconscious mind can be the primary source of your behaviour, whether you are consciously aware of it or not!

To experience the conscious and subconscious mind working together in harmony, in more coherence, is the solution to making the uncomfortable, comfortable. Hypnosis is about communicating directly with the subconscious mind and is a very powerful tool in creating positive changes, therefore resulting in a reduction or elimination of any destructive beliefs and patterns at the subconscious level. Rewiring or reprogramming your brain with powerful suggestions, is a powerful way to work below the surface and remove these old outdated programs, which can be just like roadblocks that are holding you back in your life. When these new learnings or suggestions are delivered and accepted when the brain is in hypnosis (a brainwave frequency), new neural pathways can be created.

My passion is helping you find your inner peace.

I have witnessed and experienced this modality help people in so many wonderful ways. It can:

- release pain and trauma, stress, anxiety and depression
- calm the mind and improve confidence and motivation
- increase self-esteem and self-love
- release excess weight and heal addictions
- build inner strength and resilience
- achieve certainty in achieving goals, and attract more abundance
- access your self-healing capacity
- believe in yourself and your dreams, gaining clarity and certaintyof success!

These positive changes can be achieved by working with your unconscious mind, and rewiring your mind for success. You can transform your inner critic to be your inner coach.

What brainwave frequency is hypnosis?

The realm of your subconscious is theta waves, which are frequencies present in hypnosis, deep meditation and light sleep, including the all-important REM dream state. There are five brainwave frequencies (beta, alpha, theta, delta and gamma), and each frequency is measured in cycles per second (Hz) and represents a specific level of brain activity with a unique state of consciousness.

Beta (14-40 Hz) Beta waves are associated with a heightened state of alertness, logic and critical reasoning, but can also translate into stress, anxiety, fear and restlessness. This is the normal waking consciousness.

Alpha (7.5-14 Hz) Alpha waves are the gateway to your subconscious mind and the voice of your intuition, which becomes clearer and more profound the closer you get to 7.5Hz. Alpha waves are present in the deep, physical and mental relaxation during light meditation or a daydream. This is an optimal time to program the mind for success, and it also heightens your imagination, visualisation memory, learning and concentration.

Theta (4-7.5 Hz) Theta waves are present during hypnosis, deep meditation and light sleep, including the all-important REM dream state. It is the realm of your subconsciousness. It is the Alpha–Theta brainwave pattern, from 7 Hz to 8 Hz, that is the optimal range for hypnotherapy, creative visualization, and mind programming. Your body is in deep relaxation. This level is commonly found in a hypnotised person.

Delta (0.5-4 Hz) Delta waves are experienced in deep sleep and in very deep hypnosis states, as well as in transcendental meditation. This is where awareness is fully detached and the deep sleep wave frequency is experienced. It is explained as the gateway to the universal mind and the collective unconscious. This level is important for healing and is linked with deep regeneration.

Gamma waves (above 40 Hz) Research shows that these brainwave frequencies are associated with insight and high–level information processing.

The new learnings that are created in the optimal brainwave frequency can create new neural pathways, which are new patterns of thought. When you have new positive patterns of thought, you will experience improved behaviours and more positive thinking! For instance, if you want to release excessive weight without feelings of dieting, you can program your mind to think slim, resulting in weight loss, easily and naturally. You would experience new behaviours, such as eating less junk food, reducing portion sizes or exercising more –behaviours that will help you achieve your goals. If you want to build more inner strength and resilience to meet life's challenges, you can easily and effortlessly do that.

Program your internal GPS for success

Your unconscious mind is like your internal GPS. When you program it for success, whatever that means for you, you cannot help but achieve what it is that you desire.

When you identify what you want your successful outcome to be, it is even easier to program 'your mind's GPS' for success. Hypnotherapy helps people create new neural pathways –more positive thought patterns. When we have more positive thought patterns, our behaviours are more likely to be conducive to the outcome we want.

Calming the mind and rewiring the brain

Calming the mind and breathing deeply is the single most powerful thing most people can do for their health and wellbeing.

Destressing the mind can decrease the stress hormone in the body and improve your immune system. Relaxing the mind and letting go of tensions and worries can have a wonderfully profound effect on your body, mind and health – be more present and at peace with you. Your immune system is constantly affected by the activity of your unconscious mind. Our unconscious mind looks after our body and health.

Scientific evidence that your mental state affects all the cells in your body – the mind affects the body.

Is your mind like a super highway with speeding cars and constant traffic, or is it like a beautiful relaxing drive in the countryside?

Calming the mind, slowing down the rate at which thoughts operate, can change your whole biochemistry. I have seen wonderful changes in overall health and success in life – just by calming the mind and being more present.

Constant ruminating and repetitive thinking of negative or worrying thoughts, can cause a brain to be in stress. When the brain is stressed, you can experience anxiety, depression, fatigue, low moods and memory issues, and be unable to tap into your own creativity.

You will be more successful rewiring your mind, when it is calmer and not stressed.

Your brain learns faster when it is relaxed and in a beta brainwave pattern.

The good news is, you can train your mind to be calmer and more peaceful, which results in feelings of more happiness and success!

Whether it is achieved through meditation, breathwork, hypnosis or sitting in the quietness of nature and tapping into you, you can breathe in calm and peace to ease stress and anxiety.

When we quieten the busy mind, it helps us tap into the inner part of you, the part that sometimes is not heard in the busy-ness of life. Most people have an overactive mind, and over time this can lead to feelings of lethargy, tiredness and low moods, as the brain and body experiences the stress of this overactivity.

This overactivity can also lead to memory issues, because you are not fully present in the moment. When we can bring more peace and stillness into your mind, magic can happen: your biochemistry can change and your muscles and nerves start to relax. Your mind and body can feel more balanced.

The beginnings of more peace, calm and contentment can be just thoughts away.

Most people don't realise they have the power to retrain their brains to be calmer and more successful. Hypnotherapy is a powerful way of creating better thought patterns. With hypnotherapy we are also relaxing and calming the mind as well as empowering it.

Visualise your success to create new neural pathways

You can train the brain to create a new neural pathway with visualisation and repetition. A neural pathway can be described as deep grooves or roads in our brain.

Behaviours can become automatic when our brain cells travel the same pathway, because the connection becomes stronger when these brain cells communicate frequently. This is called 'neuronal firing'.

Activities such as riding a bike and driving are examples of when new neural pathways have formed and new behaviours have developed. We can utilise creative visualisation to help form these new neural pathways.

This is where solutions focused hypnotherapy is a wonderful tool in helping to create fast behaviour change and achieve the success you desire. Calming the mind and visualising what it is you want to achieve is the beginning of creating new neural pathways.

Tips to help train your brain for success

1. Choose a goal you deeply desire – big or small

For example, if your goal is to achieve your optimal weight and body shape, you would start by visualising what that looks like for you.

2. Vividly imagine the result

- What do you look like when you have achieved this?
- What size are you?
- Turn up the colours and sounds of this picture.

3. How does it feel (really focus in on this)?

- What activities are you doing?

How are you feeling?

Are you at a special event and people are paying you compliments?

Engaging all of your senses in this visualisation exercise can start to create new neural pathways, which can lead to better behaviours for you in achieving this goal. Neural pathways are the basis of your thinking, feeling, habits and behaviours. You will experience more inner confidence about achieving your goals because your subconscious mind will absorb these amplified feelings in the images you create when you practise this exercise daily.

Thinking positive

Negative thinking, worry and fear lead your mind to think of things that you do not want in your life. Training your mind to think about what it is that you DO want in your life is one of the secrets to success.

When we focus our thoughts and feelings on happiness, we strengthen the happiness neural pathways. When we focus on thoughts and feelings of stress, we strengthen the stress neural pathways in our brain circuitry.

Changing the negative thought into a positive one can eliminate the negative thought, as your mind can only think of one thought at a time.

If you are feeling overwhelmed, you can tell yourself: 'I can keep learning and keep going. I'm doing great. I don't have to be perfect. Just taking one small step forward is actually all I need to do to get started.'

Gratitude

When we choose to focus on gratitude and appreciation, we start to train the brain to think of what we have, instead of thinking about what we lack or don't have.

A great morning or night ritual is to write in a gratitude journal.

Practice mindfulness. As you connect with your feelings and thoughts, learn how to express more gratitude and thankfulness for all you are and have. Ask yourself, what am I thankful for today? This process can help improve your physical and mental health and can also help train your brain for success.

> 'Gratitude opens the door to … the power, the wisdom, the creativity of the universe. You open the door through gratitude.' – Deepak Chopra

Practice self-love

If you are totally new to the concept of self-love, I encourage you to learn to nourish yourself.

- Do not compare yourself to others; comparison is the thief of joy.
- Start each day with a positive praise – just for you.
- Allow yourself to make mistakes.
- You are unique, and you matter. You are as unique as your fingerprint.
- You have your own unique gifts to bring into the world, and you are meant to be here.
- Celebrate your wins, big or small, and be kind to yourself.
- Follow your passion and what lights you up.
- You are special. Embrace what is different about you. Most people see in themselves what they do not like, so I encourage you to focus on what you like, and learn to love you more. There is only one YOU.

- Let go of past hurts and trauma. Forgive others and yourself.
- Your value does not decrease based on someone else's inability to see your worth. A diamond cannot see its own value in the marketplace. It just is, and it shines brightly.

If you need help in creating more positive neural pathways in your life, and want behaviours that lead you towards your goals, you can visit my website and download my *Hypnotic Mind Solutions* series, which I have created to help you achieve more happiness and success.

To your health, wealth and success.

Leanne

Leanne Kerrison

Leanne Kerrison is a clinical hypnotherapist, psychotherapist and NLP practitioner.

Leanne completed a clinical hypnotherapy diploma in Sydney, Australia, and has undertaken specialised training in advanced clinical hypnotherapy, psychotherapy and NLP.

Leanne founded Hypnotic Mind Solutions and has developed

the *Brain Training for Success* series, 'Find Your Flow – Transform Your Inner Critic to Your Inner Coach', 'Ease Anxiety Today' and 'Happy Confident You', and she continues to help people with the successful 'Think Slim Gastric Band' hypnotherapy program.

Having helped many people over the years, Leanne continues to work in private practice, helping people achieve their goals, whatever they might be.

'I help many people, including elite athletes, CEO's, entrepreneurs and business professionals, to reduce stress, increase motivation and performance, and live healthier.'

You can rewire your brain and transform you. Change how you think, feel and act, so you can create more calm and peace in your life and have more happiness, confidence and productivity.

Email: @leannekerrisonhypnotherapy
Website: www.hypnotic-mind-solutions.com & www.leannekerrison.com

DECODING YOUR MAGIC

Dr Katie Henry

You are full of limitless potential and you get to choose to ACTIVATE your potential because YOU ARE MAGIC!
– Dr Katie Henry

Maybe you are a bit like me, you know you are meant for more. How do we tap into more?

We are filled with limitless magical potential that is just waiting to be activated. How do we activate this potential? How do we activate our magic and our purpose?

The cool breeze of the lake rushes across my skin, and my feet hit the pavement in a beautiful rhythm. As I run along Lake Michigan in downtown Chicago, I feel myself in flow. A run is a place for me to find stillness and peace, to think and be present while my body moves with flow.

Although there is extraordinary effort in keeping a quick pace, it feels easy and natural. Then BOOM the peace and flow are done, it hits me! Stopping dead in my tracks, I realise I have been running my whole life! I have been running from everything: my true feelings and emotions, my truth and the life I desired. Did I even know what I wanted?

I had been running away from what everyone told me I should do or what I believed I had to do.

At that moment I was being invited to run towards my purpose, my passion, my joy … and my MAGIC!

I got back from that run perplexed because I thought, like many people, that I was living a good life. I had been an overachiever my whole life … my plate was not only full but overflowing. While working full-time as a paediatric physical therapist at the best rehab hospital in the US, I was also running a coaching business. I was healthy, had a great family, good friends, a boyfriend I loved, a spiritual practice and a social life. Yet the reality was, I was falling apart inside. I was empty, numb and exhausted. I really had been running for almost thirty years!

Have you ever felt that way? You go through your life and then all of the sudden you slow down, stop or maybe life makes you stop. You wonder: Who am I really? Is this all that life is meant to be? Is there something more for me? What is my purpose? You are NOT alone. My clients ask me these questions all the time.

You may be wondering what all of this has to do with decoding your wellness … the answer is it has everything to do with wellness.

Unfortunately, I learnt first-hand that living out of alignment with your purpose, your passion, your joy and your MAGIC (those are all the same thing) is extremely detrimental to your health and wellness.

For me, this resulted in collapsing in the elevator at work, getting in a bike accident to SLOW me down (yet I still went to work with broken fingers and my leg in a full leg splint, when my job was to teach kids how to walk … ironic right? I couldn't even walk myself), adrenal fatigue, complete burnout and a relationship completely falling apart. All of a sudden everything crumbled.

Have you ever felt like everything was falling apart or you were a total mess? Have you ever felt guilty for wanting more when things seemed pretty good?

This is the gift! We get to let the old reality go to create a new one … OUR REALITY!

Not the reality someone (insert whatever influenced you: parents, friends, a boss, society) told us we had to live. This causes us to live out of alignment. Let's choose the reality we desire to create.

We get to say yes to our MAGIC. We get to because it is a conscious choice. We get to say yes to the reality that is aligned with our soul, our purpose and our divine truth. Living in alignment with your magic not only helps you to be a happier more joyful person but also a much healthier and well person. We have forgotten that our lives are meant to be enjoyed and our bodies, minds and spirits are meant to THRIVE!

This chapter is all about how you get to decode your magic and choose to live in alignment with your purpose, your joy and your MAGIC!

The reason why so many of us seek forever to find our purpose or our magic is because we are chasing SOMEONE else's reality.

Only you get to determine your magic because it lives within you. Your magic is your essence, your soul, your spirit and your frequency. Your magic is unique to you. I am here to simply activate your magic within you. You get to do the work to identify, understand and believe in your magic. This is the beautiful journey we get to take in our human experience.

Anything another person has done is evidence of what is possible for you. Use me as an example of what's possible. I am a work in progress, and I live out everything I am teaching here on a daily basis. We get to do our best every single day and that is PERFECT!

Let's start with decoding our magic, also known as our genius and our purpose, and then we will dive into how we identify it.

Action steps we get to take to DECODE our MAGIC:

The first step is letting go of what you think you should do. Letting go and releasing the 'shoulds' will clear and create space for us, not only in our minds but also in our energy and emotions. We store and hold emotions in various parts of our bodies. If you have chronic pain or an injury that keeps coming back, it is not only a physical injury but also an emotional and energetic experience that is stored and needs to be cleared. For example, lower back problems could actually be lack of financial support, or chronic headaches could be self-criticism or fear.

Emotions are held in our bodies as well: sadness is in our lungs, fear is in our kidneys, anger in our liver (this is all Chinese medicine).

When we let go of these stories, patterns and beliefs, we also get to let go of the emotions and heavy energy as well. It is a cathartic experience, that creates space for us to be able to tap into what we desire and what our magic is. So many of us search for our purpose and our magic for so long because we cling onto these old stories, emotions and patterns. This is because that is all we know and it keeps us safe. We get to break these patterns by leaning into the resistance and the fear because, just like with our physical muscles, resistance makes us stronger and reminds us of our resilience. We get to be brave enough to let go, to trust and to believe that through the resistance we truly do get stronger!

Imagine how free you will feel when you let go of the baggage, the stories, the emotions, the pain, the trauma and the energy you've held onto for years. I can tell you from personal experience, it is the scariest thing to do yet the most liberating and freeing experience. How do we fully let go? We trust.

The next step is TRUST. Trust is one of the hardest steps for most of us because true trust is about believing in yourself before seeing it and before it becomes your reality. We get to see energetically and

FEEL the feelings we desire, and to create opportunities to trust. When you begin to trust, you begin to strengthen your intuition. Your intuition is the KEY to decoding your magic. Your intuition is your inner voice, inner knowing and, most importantly, the connection to the divine within you.

One of the simplest ways to begin to strengthen your trust is to action on your initial gut 'hit'. Try this out at a restaurant. Quickly look at the menu and see one thing that stands out to you and order it … Shut the menu and trust that you made the right choice. Start there and allow this trust to compound. Each time you listen to your intuition and to those gut feelings, you are strengthening your trust and your intuition. Remember your intuition is your direct connection to the divine and to your magic!

The final step is true belief that there is MAGIC within us, and a belief that we are meant for more and we are limitless. This goes beyond just writing out affirmations or journaling. I do fully endorse journaling and a journal prompt I have for you is: What do I choose to believe about my magic?

Full belief involves our mind, our bodies and our energy… We get to embody the belief that there is MAGIC within us. When we fully believe, we are in alignment. It becomes who we are, and then we get to embody our magic. Belief also requires leaning on support. This is where coaches, mentors and guides come into play. Belief is where you get to receive support from source, spirit, angels, guides and the universe. There are many ways to tap into this support and to access and activate this magic. I personally believe that channelling and igniting your intuition are some of the best ways to feel the universe's support and guidance, which is always present, as well to feel the magic that lies within us.

What is your magic you ask? Your MAGIC is what makes you YOU! YOU are your PURPOSE! As Dr Suess says, be the youiest you you can be. We all get to be the fullest expression of ourselves and step into our magic.

That's one of the reasons my free Facebook community is called **You are Magic:** https://www.facebook.com/groups/youaremagic

Although this is a complex topic, the best way to describe how to find your magic is to look at what comes naturally to you. Some of us feel stuck when presented with this question, because our current reality doesn't allow us to see our magic. If this is you, I invite you to reflect back on what you LOVED to do as a child (when we approached the world with wonder, curiosity and possibility). What did you love to do? What did you want to be when you grew up?

Since our magic and our purpose is physical, mental, emotional, spiritual and energetic, it is important to look at what comes naturally to you.

Examine what comes naturally to you in the following ways:

- With your senses: Which of your senses is most powerful? Sight? Sound? Smell? Taste? Touch? (This is often tied to your spiritual gifts, and if you want to learn more about this please check out the Activate your Magic program.)
- How do you enjoy interacting with others? One-to-one? In person? Over the phone? Over video chat? In written form?
- What activities do you love to do?

Identifying all of this information will help you to be able to better understand what comes naturally to you. This intertwines with your purpose and your magic.

These three MAGICAL steps will help you to not only Decode the Magic that lives within you, but to also bring more alignment into your life, your mind, your energy, your health, your finances, your relationships and your career/business, and of course it will allow you to THRIVE to your fullest potential!

Key takeaways to Decode your Magic:

- Release the 'shoulds'.
- Trust your intuition.
- Believe in MAGIC.

Together these principles will allow you to live more aligned, joyful, healthier and more magical lives. A way to begin to integrate these three steps, to trust your intuition and step into belief in your magic, is when you face a decision to put your hand on your heart and ask if what you are feeling or experiencing is true. If the answer is YES, then TRUST your intuition and those gut feelings. If the answer is NO, then you get to release that story or belief because it is NOT your truth! Your heart and your body always knows! This exercise is a perfect way to strengthen your trust.

Next steps to Decode your Magic:

Join this free training: Own your Magic with Dr Katie Henry: https://drkatiehenry.clickfunnels.com/own-your-magic

Dr Katie Henry

Dr Katie Henry is an intuitive business coach, channel, energy healer, holistic health and brain health coach, and Doctor of Physical Therapy. She is an expert in the brain, intuitive healing, energy, business and joy. Dr Katie empowers heart-centred entrepreneurs, healthcare providers and healers to infuse joy and higher consciousness into all areas of their life/ business and to tap into their magic.

Qualifications: She earned her doctorate in physical therapy from Duke University and is an expert in mindset, neuroscience and the brain. She has taught at Northwestern University's Medical School and has spoken all over the US. In addition to her formal education, she dived deep into her spiritual practice and became a spiritual teacher, yoga/meditation and reiki teacher, licensed Desire Map and Fire Starter Facilitator, EFT practitioner, author and speaker. She is a divine channel. She teaches channelling and spiritual energetics, mindset, business, mental, spiritual and physical health as well as practical action steps in your life and business ... it really is MAGIC!

She has always had spiritual gifts, even as a child, yet was told to ignore them and that they weren't real. She grew up in a religious community yet always felt like there was more. She leaned into fears and trusted herself and the divine to do some beautiful spiritual work in this world and is determined to teach others it is SAFE to be a channel for the divine. Dr Katie believes joy is our natural state and we should tap into the curiosity, wonder, fearlessness, and joy within us. Katie loves jamming to music, moving her body, especially at SoulCycle, exploring in nature, journaling, reading and daydreaming about her next travel adventure. She now lives in Austin, Texas with her husband. It's time to activate YOUR fullest potential because You are MAGIC!

Ready to activate your potential?

How you can work with me: You can work with me through one-to-one coaching, group mastermind (EMBODIED Mastermind), online courses, (including my free You are Magic Community) and through my social media content.

What I am currently working on: my podcast, the Be the Channel course (which follows the Activate your Magic program) and a new certification (that also has CEUs for my fellow healthcare providers).

Join this free training: Own your Magic with Dr Katie Henry → **https:**//drkatiehenry.clickfunnels.com/own-your-magic

Website: https://drkatiehenry.com/

Instagram: https://www.instagram.com/drkatiehenry/

Facebook: https://www.facebook.com/drkatiehenry

LinkedIn: https://www.linkedin.com/in/dr-katie-henry-21b99312/

LISTEN TO YOUR BEING

Mishel Karen

Beings is a term that describes everything energy. You exist, you radiate, you vibrate, you are a BEing in my realm.

We, as BEings, are our own healers; we innately know how to heal ourselves, to fix our own life dramas and manifest our life journey into whatever we desire. We have not listened to ourselves for so long that knowing when to listen, or what to listen to, has become difficult in this very noisy world. Our healing answers do not come to us immediately or clearly. If they did, it would be so simple and ideal. No, they come to us when we are still and in the moment, contemplating the now, being here, feeling what is happening and knowing the deeper purpose of what is happening. We seek health, wellness or answers to ailments, and the answers are being shown to us. Our body protects us and reacts with natural alerts; although in these times, we are too busy and are not listening – we are not in the moment to realise that our body has just spoken, and it is time to listen.

It only took a major conflict shock and fifty years in my human suit for me to do so.

Growing up, I had a feeling of never fitting in, not feeling 'right' around family and friends. I asked myself: Why do my actions bother them? What is wrong? Who was wrong? Why am I so unhappy? Why do I feel that my voice does not matter? Who can hear what I am trying to say? Who wants to hear it? Who needs to hear it?

These questions have been a reoccurring theme my entire life; I have looked for guidance, reaching out to 'experts' and 'gurus', hoping they could help or answer my questions, so that I would stop me feeling this way. I wanted to know, I needed to know, but my search outside of ME was fruitless, and I could never find the answers.

I spent my entire life listening to other people giving me their insight and expertise about me. Why? Why would their solution be the best for me? Why put trust in them? How could they know me when I barely knew myself?

And there was the answer! I do know ME. I have spent fifty years in this human suit, fifty years with this specimen, and I know it inside and out. I know how it thinks, feels, eats, laughs, breathes and loves. I AM its expert! The wise one is ME. It makes me laugh now that I have insight, but how could anyone or anything, possibly know ME more than ME?

I delved back to my original questioning, desperately seeking what was wrong with me. Why did I feel unhappy or dissatisfied? Was I genuinely unhappy or was I told or 'sold' the story? My hopes, dreams and expectations were blurred when my life was meshed and interwoven with many other BEings and their lives. Growing up in a strong, traditional, European family, with a rigid support system of caring, acceptance and love that is contingent on fitting in with the conventional script, I was sometimes successful at fitting in. It was not a natural state for me, but I still wanted to be loved and accepted by the people that meant the most to me.

I went looking for 'love'.

My search for love led me to Married at First Sight (MAFS), a reality television show. Unequivocally, the experiment was not successful in helping me to find love with another human. This time I was single, with a digital record of my connections with other

BEings. Rarely do we get to put ourselves in a situation where we relinquish our power of control, where our resolve is tested to see what type of BEing we are. I realised that my experiment went far deeper. I did not choose the option to belong, to align with others. I chose to stand alone, empower ME, take my unique path, walk my truth with inner strength and love my uniqueness. I took control of my mind and made the right choice to love, love ME.

Not one of us gets out of MAFS with this knowledge. It takes a lot of work, a barrage of work, on the body, mind and spirit. The 'after MAFS', the period after being on reality television but in particularly Married at First Sight, is a syndrome, a DISease (conflict active healing) in itself. No one could prepare me for this, or my experience on the show. I need to heal, see the truth, feel safe again, find love for ME. I was looking for someone to help me do this and I found ME.

My time on MAFS brought up some unresolved traumas, and I did not know how to deal with them at the time. Couple that with being in an unfamiliar environment, having an irregular filming schedule, being given non-living food choices as meals – these were prime conditions for gaining a protective layer of fat. Released and rattled physically, mentally and emotionally by this experience, I entered 2020, the year of BEing fifty. Symbolically, it was the beginning of a new chapter, the start of the next half century of my life. I was going to be fabulous before my big five-oh, and I was not going to let anything stop me! NOTHING!

Ironically, almost everything stopped me, even my body wanted to put a stop on things. It was clear that nothing was going to plan. I want my plans to go my way. I am headstrong. 2020, you are not changing my plans! It turned out 2020 changed everyone's life and plans, not just mine. The shift in energy and life as we knew it was phenomenal in 2020, and we would never go back to how it was.

But I was going to be fabulous and fifty, just in the way that it was intended to be.

In March 2020, I announced to my Instagram followers that I would be embarking on a weight loss journey. They would be able to follow my journey and keep me accountable. By June, my weight loss journey was not going so well. It was proving to be difficult to find a program I enjoyed and that worked. My morale was low, and I started to feel unwell.

My health progressively got worse over four weeks as a virus took hold of my body. I sought guidance almost daily, as my body decided to slowly give up. I became so unwell that I could barely walk a few metres. I was not eating, and I drank only the smallest amount of water. I was alone in my house, and no one was physically checking in on me. I lost all concept of time and what I should have been doing to sustain health or life. I believe I was preparing to exit this realm when a kind BEing called to check on me. When she spoke with me, she realised I was slipping into unconsciousness. The next thing I knew, I was admitted into hospital with acute kidney injury and liver inflammation … so close to the next realm. With so much to achieve in a year, I was delayed once again.

What was life trying to tell me? What was my body telling me? Why did I not see or feel the warning signs? Did I not hear the messages? Why did I need to get to this point in my life to realise I needed to stop and listen to my body to live? This was a significant moment. It was the beginning of a new mindset and attitude: cleansing and eliminating what I no longer needed in my life, what it needed to un-become.

The beginning of listening to my BEing.

One of the biggest adventures we take is the journey into ourselves, experiencing every symptom that happens to our body as a reaction to what is happening to the BEing – emotionally and spiritually. Allowing the body to heal itself is to experience the miracles of the journey. The adventure is not so much about becoming anything, it is more about un-becoming everything that is not you so you can be who you were meant to BE.

My cleansing process started with the sorting and elimination of foods. I evaluated the energy frequency of what I was putting in my body. I believe that a healthy mind, body and spirit needs healthy, happy produce that is grown and sourced with love. It is difficult to think purely and cleanly when we have toxins and chemicals running through our bodies.

My reason for cutting everything out of my diet came from my health scare. It really made me consider everything that went into my mouth. I needed a sense of what I knew to be true: my truth when I was considering the food groups. So, I systematically contemplated each matrix of living organism and how this could synergise and complement my own frequency, to determine whether it made the cut in my new 'way of life'.

When you look over my choices, it essentially breaks down to real food in its simplest form. It makes sense to let food be food. I am now conscious when I cook. I cook happy, and I know the purpose of cooking. I create with love, thinking of how the food will nurture my body. I contemplate the energy and frequency of the food and have an appreciation for all the energy.

My change in 'way of life' was not a weight loss plan, and I am not claiming to be a weight loss guru. But I know a few things about the body and food. Firstly, the body needs food. How much and what you give it determines what the human suit looks like. When I converted to listening to my BEing, I lost weight, I lost a substantial number of kilograms. And it was quite simple, the weight melted off, so it seemed, and it may happen to you, although that is not the objective.

My Rationale:

Food	Rationale	Yes/no
Vegetables	These have heaps of vitamins and minerals. I enjoy eating nearly every type of vegetable.	✓
Fruit	These have the same nutritious value as vegetables, and they make me feel incredibly happy. Fruit has a positive effect on most people's moods.	✓
Eggs	Eggs are the super food for so many pathogens and bacteria. Supplying nutrition for these bad guys was not in my plan.	✗
Meat	I am an omnivore; I will limit my intake.	✓
Fish	A source of nutrition. I will eat oily fish. As I am eliminating oil this will be my source of oils.	✓
Oils	The process to extract oils uses chemicals and heating; this does not seem natural.	✗
Lard	Use for cooking, when needed. It was used by my Baba (grandmother).	✓
Herbs	Use for flavour; I have so many growing in my garden.	✓
Nuts and seeds	Not right now, but eventually.	✗
Dairy	This is too processed; I do not require any nutrients from dairy that I cannot source from vegetables.	✗
Processed foods	If it comes out of a packet, I will not eat it.	✗
Chocolate	I am not huge chocolate fan, but if I think I need it, I can always have carob made from 80% or higher cocoa.	✓
Alcohol	I did not have to ask myself this as I barely ever drink. But I appreciate that most people saw me drink copious amounts of wine. Aahhh reality television.	✗

The focus of the plan was my health and wellbeing, not my weight. It included mindful, or intuitive eating. It was about listening to my body and teaching myself to eat in response to my own internal cues of hunger, fullness and appetite, rather than formally restricting the type or amount of food eaten. It was loving what I have, and BEing 'love'.

You can access the full plan if you think this 'way of life' would assist you, join me on my Weight Wellness Program at: www.mishelkaren.com.

Elimination

Elimination involves getting rid of processed foods and toxins and removing and transforming stored resentment and toxic emotions that do not serve you. Eliminating physical toxins was only doing half the job. With any good detox or purge, it is necessary to purge emotionally and spiritually as well. It goes hand in hand – elimination of toxins and transforming toxic emotions, dumping of junk food and dumping of resentment, cleaning out the cupboard and cleaning out stored mental patterns. Every physical clearing or action has an emotional or metaphysical clearing; clearing one realm, does not work without clearing the other. I made room for the new ways by cleaning out the old ways first.

First stop was the refrigerator, and the clearing was ruthless. If it did not assist in my 'way of life' outlook, it took up space, valuable space that I needed for fresh fruits, vegetables and fresh meat. Next, the pantry was hit by hurricane Mishel, and it was left looking like an empty bookshelf. It sustained the most damage on that day, as so much of our food sources have been processed, packaged and stored, ready to be consumed in a few years' time. Processed food does not sound as inviting when you realise that it can sit in your pantry for years and still be ready for consumption.

Journaling was key at this time. I kept an accurate record of how I felt doing the elimination process: an emotional activity with many poignant breakthroughs. I transformed the old negative ways that caused pain, let go of my need to be a victim and expanded my personal transformation.

Support and Nurture

With any transformation or elimination, our BEing needs love and support. I needed to support my mind, body and spirit in ways that felt right for me. I have included my support and nurture rituals at the end of this chapter. My Healy is never very far from my reach.

We need a healthy level of selfishness to accomplish what is beneficial for each one of us. On the list I have provided, I have included enough variation for the busiest individual but also enough for those of us that need more to do. We know instinctively when we are at one with life and love, these are not activities we would continue to do just for the sake of it.

The Internal Critic

At some stage in my life, I engaged the services of the 'internal critic', who kept me in line by telling me I was not okay. The internal critic's voice got stronger when I saw what the media portrayed as a vision of perfection or when I visited the doctor or heard a loved one's voice tell me I needed to improve on how I looked. This unconscious agreement that I made with internal critic so long ago, was taking up so much of my energy and my life force, as I tried to improve myself with every means and resource at my disposal, and yet I still felt like

I needed fixing. I felt better for a little while but the cycle was tiring and never ending. I realised I needed to accept myself, love myself, to not question why or how or if, just love me and move on. This unconditional love for yourself is a love that remains regardless of what you have done, said, worn, eaten, felt; it is a love that loves your quirks and conditions, and a love that makes you smile – true LOVE.

It is my wish that everyone knows that healing is within them and they too can 'Listen to their Being' and heal themselves. I would like to tell you that this is an easy journey and that there is a heap of support along the way, but neither of these are true. There will be people to pick you up when you fall but you need to do the hard work. You may suffer, and each of us suffers to different degrees during our journey. Legitimate suffering is necessary, as it is when we suffer that we grow. Just like when rainbows appear after storms, our ever-expanding glory and intangible essence explodes into ever expanding knowing.

My biggest challenge was locating the channel that allowed me to receive my frequency to transmit my consciousness and be able to 'Listen to my Being', and then, once found, having the courage to believe and trust. Arriving at this consciousness requires a pureness, a cleansing, allowing only high frequency nourishment, whether that be of food, water and love or a high frequency of mind, body and spirit nutrients. I have shared my path in detail to all BEings, I encourage you to follow my path or adapt what I did to gain your own wisdom.

Ultimately, it took MAFS – being exposed on television – for me to realise that other people saw me, that other people 'knew me' and could relate to me; I did not need the public approval, but knowing that I had it, confirmed in my mind that I am perfectly imperfect, the most beautiful version of me.

I am the only authority in my life. I live in the vibration of my energy field. I accept myself with my imperfections as uniqueness, a BEing, a love.

Blessings to all, love and light,
Mishel

Support and Nurture plus Healy Frequency

MIND		
	Daily affirmations of love	Speak to yourself with the energy of love. Use the energy of love vibration with your daily affirmations as you repeat them to yourself first thing in the morning.
PURE	Detox on all levels	I want to be clean and pure. My thinking is PURE.
	Meditations	Use a method that you find simple and reliable – YouTube has a vast selection.
DIGEST ALL	Detox of intestines, stomach, pancreas, and gallbladder.	I can digest all I experienced in my life.
GO TO THE ROOTS	Harmonise mental, emotional and bio-chemical processes.	I can feel my roots and use this resource to grow.
	Mindfulness	Practice the Art of Mindfulness – Five senses Grounding Activity (see Intention Cards).
RELAX	Relaxation	I am relaxed and calm
BEING	Balancing emotions	I am calm and content

BODY		
	Exercise	Move your body – walk, dance, swim, run.
BALANCE	Kidney, circulation, lymphatic system, hormones	My energy organs are working perfectly
	Stretch	Try to stretch a few times a week: yoga, Pilates or stretches.
	Eat well	Let food be food. Prepare your body with good, fresh nutritious food. Where possible grow your own.
CARE	Balance body functions	I eat and drink healthily
DIGEST ALL Listen to your body	Detox of intestines, stomach, pancreas, and gallbladder.	I can digest all I experienced in my life.

SPIRIT		
	Adopt a Self-Care Ritual	Give yourself permission to love and care for yourself. Take a bath, a sun bath – be energised by the sun, or spend time in nature.
COHERENCE	LOVE	Include LOVE frequency in your daily vibration.
	Dream Journal	Start by trying to remember your dreams. Write them down and then look for the messages your subconscious mind is communicating with you in your dreams.
RELEASE	Release pain and acidity	I let go of blockages
	Gratitude Practice	Living gratefully – Express gratitude in any manner.

Mishel Karen

Hello, I am Mishel Karen. You may know and love me, as the witty and playful participant on *Married at First Sight Australia,* Season 7. Determined to meet the love of my life, 'my true loves kiss', I entered the experiment, and I married a stranger on a reality television show. The experiment did not have the result I expected or desired. Rather it held a far greater gift, one that would be of far greater significance than I could ever have imagined.

I am a naturopath and educator. I have worked in health, wellness and the education sector for nearly thirty years. I have dedicated years of study to the fields of naturopathy, health, pharmaceuticals, energy, healing, mindset and education. My career as a businesswoman in the education arena was cut short when I had tumours removed from my vocal cords and I lost my voice. My resilience in this type of situation has never let me down. I have a natural knack of picking up the pieces and rebuilding and recreating as something better – it is a recurring theme in my life.

I have continued to dedicate working in all areas of wellbeing and to work on myself, expanding my awareness of mind, body and spirit. Working on my own health – body, mind, and psyche – I uncovered real freedom and empowerment. I found reuniting with my true self had a transformational side effect – the revelation of my

Inner Goddexx and a new sense of freedom and empowerment. This is the life that I want for every BEing: a lifestyle that promotes love, kindness, health, and wellbeing.

My wish is that you realise healing is within you, and that you too can Listen to your BEing and heal yourself.

Let me join you on your journey ...

It is my goal to join you on your journey to health, wellness, weight acceptance and self-awareness. I will support you with the knowledge and motivation you need to reclaim your power, so you can reunite with your true self, glow with self-acceptance and love yourself unconditionally. This ability, I believe, is not in a tablet or even in the hands of a doctor or master guru, it lies in the hands of a higher BEing –YOU.

Website: www.mishelkaren.com.au
Instagram: mishel_meshes https://www.instagram.com/mishel_meshes/
Facebook: Mishel Karen https://www.facebook.com/mishelkaren.mesh
LinkedIn: Mishel Karen https://www.linkedin.com/in/mishel-karen-2176511ab?lipi=urn%3Ali%3Apage%3Ad_flagship3_profile_view_base_contact_details%3Bp28lhNsQQaSeR9KP3jGQ5Q%3D%3D

DECODE YOUR HEART

INTRODUCTION

Tracey Jewel

When our heart is open, everything
we do becomes love.

– Mimi Novic

The messages and thoughts that we give ourselves directly impact how we feel. You would have heard the saying many times before 'Treat yourself like you would treat somebody you love.' I don't know about you, but for me that's easier said than done! Especially when an open heart has been burnt, broken or battered. I've learnt through many broken hearts (and breaking my own heart too!) that decoding your heart starts with you and self-love. It means letting go of negative self-talk and learning to nourish yourself with kind, compassionate thoughts and expressions – even if you have to fake it at first.

How many times have you heard the phrase 'just be yourself?'. While that sounds great, few of us actually know what it means to do so. Are we true to ourselves when we let go of the stories and judgement we've placed on ourselves? Does it require practice to connect with one's sense of self? If you're unsure, the chapters that follow and the tips below can help you discover the true meaning behind this phrase so that you can actually be yourself.

Connect with Your Inner Child

If you look at children, you'll see they tend to live in the moment and care for nothing more than what's in front of them. Nothing has taught me this level of purity more than becoming a mum a second time. Children are free, unrestricted and nonconforming. They're happy because they're true to themselves. It's time to embrace your inner child.

Define Yourself

You can't ever expect to be yourself if you don't know or accept who you are. To be yourself, you have to know yourself. Learn what you like and value in life. Examine your life's choices. If you want to try something new, try and learn by trial and error. If you need some extra guidance, taking a personality test can be an excellent tool to point you in the right direction. Finding the right people and support systems to surround yourself with is also essential on this journey, so that you can feel safe, secure and supported, no matter what.

Stop Thinking About How Others Perceive You

Some people will inevitably like you, and some won't. We must accept this fact of life and move on. Don't push yourself to be wittier or funnier to appease how others view you; you'll only end up doubting your sense of worth. Learn to let go. You cannot afford to live life constantly asking yourself whether you are intelligent, thin or popular enough to become part of a community. You are already worth it.

Listen to Your Thoughts

Learn to become an observer of your own thoughts and the ins and outs of your inner world. Distancing yourself from your thoughts is not easy, but it will help you become more aware of the quality of your thinking. Allow yourself one to two minutes a day for contemplation. In these reflective states, you might find your beliefs about yourself have been handed down to you by other people. Letting go of these beliefs and aligning yourself with the present moment is how you'll reveal your true nature. In doing so, you allow yourself to grow and become someone else with each passing moment, year and decade.

Follow Your Gut

Trust yourself, and you'll begin to *be* yourself. Your intuition is uniquely yours, and by listening to it, you'll begin to connect with your innermost self. So often, we ignore our intuition because we feel obligated to others and their sense of happiness. Give yourself enough attention, follow these little urges you previously ignored; step out of your comfort zone, and seek your own pleasures. It is here that you'll find yourself.

Be Honest with Yourself

Nobody is perfect. We are all continuously growing, changing and evolving. Your faults aren't something you should hide. Nor should you pretend they don't exist. Insecurity and false beliefs that prompt you to hide an aspect of your personality from the world can leave you feeling disconnected from yourself. You must come to terms with who you are, accepting all your imperfections. Tolerance can transform quirks into characteristics that get you closer to feeling and being who you really are.

Use these methods and the ones that follow to discover and cultivate your connection with yourself. They can help you make better decisions and learn to never compromise on the values you hold most dear; and others, too, will learn to appreciate this level of authenticity.

INTUITION – YOUR PATH TO ULTIMATE HEALTH, WEALTH AND FREEDOM

Sarah Jane Blackah

Your frequency is your future.

How was it that after a twelve-year successful career in the health, freedom and lifestyle industry, I found myself being prescribed anti-depressants for an 'incurable' women's mental health and hormone condition call PMDD.

It didn't make sense. I had done ALL the things ... Like, honestly, all of them – yoga teacher training, life coaching, NLP practitioner training, creating multiple six-figure health and freedom lifestyle-based businesses, women's embodiment facilitator, travelling the world and training under every guru in the personal development space I could find.

I had fluffed my chakras, had my 'eat pray' moments with Tarzan in the Bali jungle, taken plant medicine, reiki, breathwork classes, danced like no one else's business. I had tried vegan, paleo, Keto, shakes, Chinese medicines, herbs, healers, fasting, shadow work, jade eggs ... ALL OF THE THINGS!

Yet there I was with all this knowledge and experience, back home with my parents at thirty-five, depressed, unwell and broke, thinking 'where the fuck did I go wrong?'

Surely by now I would have figured out a way to have my own health and life on track?

Staring at the pack of anti-depressants I had been handed by an intelligent female doctor at our family clinic, I thought to myself, 'This goes against everything I believe.' In the same breath, I was desperate and open to try anything, as the swings of my cycle had grinded me down to a hopeless mess. I was finding it challenging to gain an ounce of inspiration or good reason to be here anymore: a frequent feeling at the time.

The day I received the prescription, was also the day a book I had ordered arrived: *The Secrets of Natural Success*. 'Another bullshit book telling me how I can change to live the life of my dreams,' I thought to myself. I wasn't having a bar of it in the mood I was in, even though I had previously really enjoyed the writer's perspectives.

So I took the damn pills ... for three days. It did not go down so well.

I remember being in the back of a cinema with my parents (the only people who would hang out with me at the time) watching *Rocket Man*, and I had to leave because I hyperventilated while crying. I mean, it wasn't the best movie. But it wasn't that bad. :)

I returned home that night with two very worried parents, and I made a commitment to myself that I wasn't going down that road any longer. I would find a way to get my health and life back on track, even though I thought I had exhausted all the options and I had no idea how.

The following day, I sat at home feeling apathetic, when the book caught my eye again. This time I picked it up and started reading.

Several chapters in, I came across a story that was a fundamental turning point in my downward spiral of ill health and finances.

In the book the author shared his story of how he had an undiagnosable disease, that after ten years had left him eating boiled cabbage, stick thin and on his death bed. He said that after a priest had visited him at the hospital to give him his last blessings and prepare him to make the crossover, he went for a walk in the park. There he met a very healthy, fit, vibrant man who sat next to him on the park bench and not only empathised with his condition but proceeded to share that he too had suffered from the same thing and in fact had a cure – 'Enjoy a glass of red wine, eat some red meat and smoke a few cigarettes each day.'

And in that moment … I WAS FREE.

I knew that the prescription of meat and wine wasn't about protein, iron or antioxidants. It was about freedom. It was about liberation. It was about bringing awareness to where I had been orienting from most of my life, which was putting the power outside of myself: giving my power away to authorities and experts rather than trusting my own knowing and body wisdom to simply get on with enjoying my life.

I knew I had a choice here. I could go all in on the principles I was uncovering, or stay looping in the medical and wellness systems that were keeping me disempowered. So I went all in. I ordered a bottle of red, cooked myself a delicious dinner and started to get excited about life again.

It wasn't an instant cure. I had to rewire my focus and shift from being a victim of my circumstances to a powerful creator of my reality. I realised that my ill health wasn't so much about what I was eating or how long I was chanting or meditating for each day, it was about where I was coming from. It was where I had been orienting from my whole life.

I started to realise how the ill health and even the 'success' I had achieved, was actually coming from a place of perceived inadequacy: that there was something about me that I need to fix or compensate for. I had made my life about resolving my identity, which had been the source of my suffering.

And it was exhausting.

With the guidance of an intuitive mentor, I reconnected with a clear vision for my life and true end results that I would love to create. It felt wild, free and inspiring. The best part was that I got to throw out the rule book, let go of the how and allow life to show me the pathway to create it.

And that it did.

Within a number of weeks I had an intuitive hit to call one of my best long-term friends and biz partners who I hadn't spoken to in several months, and we arranged a catch up.

When I arrived at her apartment and sat down, I noticed she had a spark about her: something I couldn't quite describe that had a blend of mystery and magic. As I shared my roller coaster journey, she sat there listening with a smile on her face.

'It's here,' she said.

'What's here?' I thought to myself.

She showed me a small bio-resonance device we had been imagining during our twelve-year journey in our health and wellness careers together. Straight away I had another of those intuitive hits – a big YES coming from somewhere deep within.

That was the second turning point.

This little device went on to become the tool for freedom for my health and wealth, beyond what I thought was possible. I went on to tour around Australia sharing my story. I moved to Bali, the place I love most. I had my biggest financial months ever, started a global women's movement and impacted many thousands of lives. But beyond all of that, I felt a joy for life.

One of my favourite sayings about intuition is this: 'At first it is a feather, then it is a brick and then it is a fucking truck.'

I had the truck. Many people have the truck. But we don't need the truck.

I became committed to educating people, particularly women, about the power of alchemy and intuition as a way to overcome dogma, struggle and limitation so as to be the leaders of their own life.

The principles that I went on to study and teach became the foundations of my life and impacted all of those around me. This wasn't intuition coming from a 'woo woo' place. These were principles of alchemy grounded in deep wisdom that all the great poets, inventors, creators, entrepreneurs and revolutionary leaders have known throughout history. It is a combination of science and art, a deep connection to truth and to one's own existence.

You see, the cure for being fat is not to lose weight. The antidote for being broke is not to just get rich. The way to overcome being lonely is not to go out and find a partner. They are two different ends of the same energetic spectrum. The secret to really shift out of any problem in our life is to come from a higher frequency and vision. We must connect to the very things that bring us alive.

This is where intuition comes in. It moves us from the lower frequencies to the higher. It takes us from the limitations of mind that can only make decisions based on what it knows, to the infinite possibilities of the heart that has access to everything through all time and space.

When you learn how to master the realm of intuition, it takes you from the mundane to the magic. You learn how to bring to life your most beautiful vision. It asks you to trust, create, be bold and stretch your edges to see what you're made of, which is why so many ignore it. It asks us to live in the mystery of the unknown.

We have three choices in life. We can ignore our soul's calling or intuition, we can dull it down, which is where most people play, or we can go for the fullness of our hearts and what we would love to create in the world.

Our level of joy, that deeply fulfilling kind of joy I believe we are here to experience with our time on earth, is dependent on how aligned we are with our true nature and purpose. Intuition is the compass that is steering that alignment ship.

Don't get me wrong that doesn't mean it's all light, love and rainbows. Far from it. When you start following your intuition to create what you love, it can get a little messy. You will experience creative tension. Your limiting beliefs will come up and it will feel much more comfortable to resort back to the mind's realm of safety and the known. But that is not where your creative genius resides. That isn't where the magic lives. That's not the real solution to your 'problems' So let's talk about intuition. What is it and how do we access it?

I'm glad you asked.

Intuition can be defined as: 'what the mind apprehends before the rationalisation'. To understand it further we need to understand the different modes of awareness and how we actually create our reality. We have all heard the saying 'what we focus on expands', however, most of the time what we think we are focused on is not actually what we are focused on.

DIFFERENT ASPECTS OF CONSCIOUSNESS.

- super consciousness
- self-conscious
- subconscious (creates your reality)
- unconscious

The name of the game is to become a conscious creator of our reality by having awareness over where we are coming from. We are either coming from our unconscious beliefs and spending our life trying to resolve or compensate for them (this could look like blaming, withdrawing, talking yourself out of things, giving up, addictive behaviour, seeking validation), or we are coming from our superconscious (pure creative spirit) that is free from conditioning and can guide us to create what we love.

The ultimate questions is: What aspect of our consciousness has the most power? The subconscious is neutral. It doesn't care what it creates. It just creates what you give focus and power to.

When I was ill, I was giving power to being ill and depressed. I was spending my time doing things a depressed and in debt person would do. I was lying in bed, seeking out the opinion of different doctors, isolating, taking pills and not working or contributing to society in a meaningful way. So my subconscious got the message that I was a sick, broke person and created that reality.

On the other hand, when I started to put the focus and power into what I would love and took daily inspired action towards my visions and dreams, I started attracting the opportunities, people, resources, experiences and ideas to bring that reality into existence. My subconscious started to get the message that I was a person who had energy, purpose and power.

It only takes us to tip the power balance 51 per cent in favour of our super conscious voice (our intuition), to start seeing a new set of results in our life.

So how do we more intentionally start to access this quieter, intuitive voice over the noise in our minds? With three very simple steps:

- innocence
- observing what is obvious
- making it up.

As children we are very connected to our innocence. Hence children are naturally tapped into their intuition and genius. It is only through years of conditioning –'this is right, this is wrong, this is good, this is bad' – that we lose connection. So the first step to going beyond the limitations of the mind is to stop trying to make sense of the world and figure out 'how it is', and return to our childlike 'in no sense' to discover our truth. That means intentionally letting go of everything we think we know and being in a state of curiosity.

The second step is to observe what is obvious about whatever topic we want clarity or truth about. We always start by choosing to serve the highest good and then can tune into the truth of our vision, our genius or any other topic we want insight into. The first thing that is obvious is our intuitive voice speaking to us.

The language of intuition is different to the language of the mind. It often speaks to us through symbols, words, feelings, colours or visions, and it speaks to everyone slightly differently. The important thing is not the symbol, but what is obvious about it and what it means to you.

Which leads into the third step of intuition which is that you make it up. Yep, that is correct. You just make it up. You let your imagination play and tell you a story about what the symbol or sensation or visual means. The ironic thing is, the more you allow your imagination to run wild, the more accurate and truthful it becomes. The imagination is the language of the soul. You can feel it. The truth has a ring to it. It has a frequency: a higher, creative frequency. When we let ourselves be guided by this higher frequency, we start to experience a whole new reality.

I want to close this chapter by reminding you that you are a powerful creator of your reality. Life gets to be a game. We get to make it up and play by a new set of rules. My wish for you is that you choose to lead your life guided by your intuition, because it's the path to pretty much everything – everything in life that is really worth having, that is!

Sarah Jane Blackah

Sarah is a female leadership mentor, multiple six-figure Freedom Lifestyle Creator and intuitive.

She is here to create a new paradigm in feminine leadership – one where women can say 'screw it' to the norms and access their own intuitive wisdom to break through conditioning and create what they love.

Sarah brings together her ten plus years of experience and studies in the world of transformation, business, health and freedom lifestyles, women's embodiment and advanced intuition, in order to support women to love their true nature and purpose while having a lot of fun along the way.

Instagram: Sarah Blackah
Facebook: Sarah Blackah
Email: Sarahjblackah@gmail.com
WhatsApp: +62812 3755 8952

SEEDS OF SELF LOVE

Arielle Delescaut

The Healer you have been looking for is your own courage to know and love yourself completely.
– Yung Pueblo

I have a passion for growth and transformation, even if my life journey hasn't always been flowing and easy. Since childhood, like many of us, I was faced with family challenges, a huge feeling of insecurity and low self-esteem. So, I grew up as a disconnected and angry person, driven by negativity, self-victimisation and self-sabotage. I didn't know at the time that I was just surviving, not living.

I was living in Australia and I was feeling very homesick and sad. Two years after my son was born, I was diagnosed with post-natal depression. I was convinced that my unhappiness was due to my homesickness, until I realised many years later that the only home I was missing was mine. Following the diagnosis, I was given an anti-depressant to 'fix' me, but the only thing the treatment was doing was numbing me on the inside, making me feel even more lost and more disconnected. So, my husband (at that time) and I sold all our possessions and moved back to France with our two children, where we lived for nearly four years.

When we arrived in France, I put my pills in the bin with a strong sense of relief. Straight after I was introduced to a kinesiologist, who later became my friend. Of course, I had no idea of what kinesiology was at the time, but I was completely trusting of the process and quickly got blown away by the power of it and how fast I was moving forward. A new world of hope was opening up, and from that day there was no turning back. This is how I embarked on my healing journey.

When we came back to Australia, four years later, I knew I had found my path, and I started studying kinesiology. I was very excited with the idea of helping people. It had helped me, and I was ready to give all of that goodness back.

I knew what my life purpose was: helping others to find themselves, grow, be empowered and achieve the life they truly deserved. Once I understood the origin of my emotional pain, my spiritual journey really began. I was able to re-connect within, accept my past, make peace with it and embrace my personal story. Without knowing it, I was on my way to discovering the gift of self-love.

To be human is to love and to love is to live.

What is love?

Love is the source of all life. Love is the central story of our bodies. Love surpasses everything.

The heart is the first thing that is heard in the mother's womb to show there is life, and the heart is the last thing to stop beating as we pass over. Everything we go through in life is shaping our heart, whether we decide to open it or not.

True love is pure and unconditional. It's the kind of love that is given freely without expecting anything in return. It doesn't have a colour, a gender, a shape or an age, and it doesn't calculate time and distance. It's pure energy and can be created and generated in an infinite way.

Your heart space is a refuge, a sanctuary, a sacred treasure. It is your very own unique heritage, and like any other treasure, it is precious and needs to be nurtured. It is what brings light into your life and what makes you remember who you are. It is from this sanctuary that we tune in and listen to the whispers of our soul, and it is from where we can manifest our inner purpose, away from the ego.

I believe that healing your heart space should be made a priority, even when that requires courage, strength, bravery, vision, patience, vulnerability, trust and humility.

The heart space is an energy centre called a chakra. A chakra is a Sanskrit word that translates as 'spinning disc' or 'wheel'. Our chakra system carries our life force and is surrounded by our aura. Life force is the non-physical vitality that gives life to all living things. This energy flow has been identified by many different cultures as chi, ki, prana, grace, white light, spirit and quantum field.

The heart chakra is the centre of the system, the gateway to the higher chakras that connect to the soul self and spirit self. The main role of the heart chakra is to help us develop self-acceptance, self-love, balanced relationships, intimacy, compassion, love and the right to love and be loved.

What sets our perception of love?

There is not one person who hasn't been through suffering, and a lot of our wounds have been passed down from our ancestors – from generation to generation. So, if your parents never explored the idea of healing their wounds, it's more than likely you inherited some of them as early as the womb stage, as a cellular memory.

We are born with pure love, joy and wonder. We are not born doubting or judging ourselves, judging others, or with shame, guilt, anxiety or depression. We learnt it as we grew up from our parents, society or any form of authority figure, and this is how our unconscious mind starts to create our belief system. This, combined with our inherited wounds, is the script of our personal story and how we perceive love is created.

When I was trapped with my post-natal depression, I was dealing with so many mixed emotions that I was overwhelmed, no matter what the feeling was. Anger was always my 'go to' emotion. It made me feel alive … I could feel something … I had things to say and complain about! What I didn't realise at that time was that emotion is toxic and, instead of making me 'feel' in the true sense of feeling, it was covering the deep wounds from my childhood and disconnecting me from my true essence. As a result, I was constantly rejecting myself and others around me.

When we act from a place of pain and suffering, we aren't operating from our highest potential. We create separation and isolation from ourselves and others.

Why is self-love so important?

The fundamental purpose of human nature is to love and to be loved. This is why love/connection has been classified as one of our six basic human needs. It's not just a want, it's a profound need that serves as the basis of every choice we make.

Whilst this profound human need is present in all of us, the majority of us struggle to make sense of it and tune into it, leaving us with a feeling of disempowerment. When you settle in this state of disempowerment, it keeps you in victim consciousness and influences how you view yourself and your relationships with others. It even impacts every decision you make, and therefore how you create your reality now and in the future.

Tuning into the love vibration will lift you to a higher state of consciousness. Your energy will resonate at a higher vibration, and it will give you a far greater perspective on your life and the wider consciousness. Your heart will expand to greater joy and harmony, and you will be able to express the qualities of forgiveness, tolerance, compassion, joy, creativity, generosity, abundance and respect.

How do we cultivate self-love?

1 – Awareness

You can't change what you don't understand.

Awareness is the state of being conscious of something – to know, to perceive and to feel. It is also the first step to any change.

To recognise the pain, to be there for it, hold it, acknowledge it, to give it space is the only way to transmute it and heal it.

2 – Self-acceptance

Self-acceptance starts with overcoming how you've been programmed in childhood and embracing your own story: where you come from, your family history, the positive as well as the negative. It's accepting your inheritance as a complete part of who you are and learning to make peace with it.

The reconciliation process in my own story and the realisation that it was okay not to be perfect, were key to my healing journey.

As a child, I was raised in an environment where perfection was a huge expectation. So, in my early childhood I created the limiting belief that in order to be accepted and loved, I had to be perfect. It was only later in life that I became aware of this pattern. Not only had I huge expectations about myself, but from others too. The day

I understood that perfection was an illusion and didn't really exist in our human dimension, was the day I started to let go of my expectations, bit by bit.

The reality is that we all have a very unique way of seeing perfection … all of us. My parents' definition was different to mine, mine is different to my children's and pretty much every single human being on earth.

It's through our imperfection that we make mistakes, and it's through our mistakes that we learn the precious lessons life has to teach us.

In summary, self-acceptance does not depend on your external circumstances, nor on your successes or achievements. It is being able to accept the good and bad about yourself and not compromise on your self-worth. It is stopping searching outside of yourself for what you already have within.

When you practice radical and unconditional self-acceptance, you can begin to embrace your authentic self and love yourself.

My wish for you is to start feeding yourself from this high energy that is love. It is time to thrive instead of survive. It is time to nurture the sacred space of your heart, and it is time to heal your wounds. It is time to spread the seeds of love, and as you do, you will heal yourself, heal Mother Earth and heal those around you.

> Albert Einstein, in one of his letters to his daughter said: 'We all have a tiny but powerful love generator within us. It's just waiting for us. We need to learn to give and receive this universal energy as it can conquer and transform everything.'

WELLNESS TIPS

Give yourself permission: You're the captain of your ship. Start your day by giving yourself permission. The only person who knows what is right for you is YOU. Don't wait for people to give you permission to be, to feel, to make a decision, to take some action.

Be thankful: Practice gratitude for each experience, be it positive or negative. Some experiences aren't here to make us feel good, they come our way for us to learn and grow. Welcome the lesson and acknowledge it as an opportunity for growth and transformation.

Support yourself: Check-in daily and do one thing that YOU love to re-ignite joy, passion and flow.

Choose freedom and empowerment: When feeling trapped with a situation or an emotion, remove yourself from victim consciousness with this mantra: I ALWAYS have a choice.

Journal: You aren't your thoughts. This is a powerful exercise you can do anytime, anywhere. If you don't have a pen and paper, use your phone and write down how you're feeling – unfiltered. Don't judge it, welcome it and let it go.

Ground yourself: Connect with nature. Walk barefoot on grass, listen to the wind, look at the clouds, hug a tree, smell a flower. If you can't do all of this in nature, use a pure essential oil as they come from Mother Earth and carry its vibration.

Forgive: Every mistake you make is a gift, and every time you learn from a relationship is a blessing. Close your eyes, think about the person you want to forgive, it can even be yourself. Tell her 'I forgive you, please forgive me.'

I know it's not easy to change your life, but I also know it's much harder not to. It's never too late to rewrite your personal story, and my mission is to take you from stuck to flow.

If my words resonate with you, and you would like to take the next step to self-love and self-acceptance, please get in touch with me. I offer individual sessions as well as tailor-made coaching and healing programs.

Find your positive and negative skills! Get your free life path numerology reading here: ariellewellness.com

I look forward to supporting you, one step at a time.

Arielle Delescaut

Arielle Delescaut has a passion for growth and transformation, and she believes that true self-healing requires courage, strength, bravery, vision, patience, tenacity, vulnerability, depth, trust and humility.

Her French culture blended with the Australian way of life has made her create her very own signature in the healing world.

Through her personal story and the many lessons she has learnt, she invites you to listen from the soul and tune into your inner essence – to find YOU. She encourages you and guides you to make peace with your past, re-write your own story and befriend your soul.

Her teachings are based on unconditional self-acceptance, compassion and forgiveness. Her engaging and honest style of communication has helped hundreds of people in Europe and Australia to find their way back to self-commitment and connection.

She has created her own self-love coaching program and is currently working on a women's practitioner retreat that encompasses her professional knowledge and life experience along with her spiritual connection to the invisible realms.

Join Arielle Delescaut as she shares how self-love and self-acceptance will help you overcome any limiting beliefs created in your unconscious mind since childhood. When you give yourself permission to once and for all embrace who you unconditionally are, you will awaken to the life of your dreams.

Qualifications:

- Diploma of Kinesiology
- Reiki Master
- TimeLine Reset Coach
- Past Life Regression Practitioner
- Family Freedom Protocol Practitioner

Website: ariellewellness.com
Email: hello@ariellewellness.com
Facebook: facebook.com/ariellewellness
Instagram: @arielle.wellness

HOW TO CONNECT AND SHOW UP AS YOUR MOST AUTHENTIC SELF

Heidi Arambula

It's never too late to add to who you are!

– Heidi Arambula

All of my life I knew my divine purpose was to be a mother. I was blessed with a loving mother and knew I wanted to be like her. She was beautiful, soft and had the most loving smile.

I got married at the young age of nineteen, and I held my firstborn son, Marcus James, for the first time just a couple of months after my twenty-first birthday. It was in November of 1996 when I learned how to love in a way that was new to me. I was surprised it felt different and so perfect. It was a joy so deep within me. It was the purest form of love I'd felt, and I knew I would do anything for Marcus James. Over the next nine years, I was fortunate enough to give birth to three more beautiful souls: Rachel Mae, Annie Marie and Christian Joseph. They are my reason why.

What I didn't see coming was going through a divorce after twelve years of marriage and leaving the church I was raised in. This season was so incredibly painful. I was in the depths of despair. Occasionally I would take a Benadryl at night to quiet my mind and drift into a deeper sleep. This would give me a brief relief from my intense feelings. My family was disappointed in me. I hurt my ex-husband. He hurt me. My children had a new reality and it pained me that their sweet little hearts hurt. Just so much sadness surrounded us. My soul was on fire and I desperately needed a reprieve.

Having been raised in a devout faith with strict rules, every thought and action I made was wrapped up in the teachings within my religion. My life suddenly had other options I never would have imagined for myself before. I examined everything on a different level. Who am I? What do I like? Do I believe in a higher power? Even though I was going against the things I was taught, I knew I was good and wanted to prove myself. I knew I needed to add to who I was.

I always felt lucky to be able to stay home with my children, but now the stark reality of me becoming a single mom was right in front of me and all the responsibilities that come along with that. I had to find a job. I was scared! I didn't have a formal education and not a lot of real-world job experience. With much hemming and hawing, talking it through with family and friends, I decided to go to laser technical school. I sobbed after my first day of class because I felt so inadequate. The didactics challenged me so much, but I continued to study and aced all of my exams.

When it came to the practical application, I really started to shine. I got the techniques down and found it easy to put others at ease while doing procedures. I was pretty dang good at it and building that confidence was such a big part of my healing and growth.

I got my first job in aesthetic lasers fourteen days post-graduation. Things were looking up. I was at that job for eighteen months before I was recruited for a higher-paying job. I stayed with that company for five years. I only left because I was ready to give birth to my bonus baby, Lincoln Thomas.

Five years prior to Lincoln being born, I met my husband, Ricky. My children and I were invited to my neighbour's son's birthday party. I never would have guessed I would meet my future husband there. We were married three years later. I would describe my husband as a man who is good to his core. He loves me and my children so much. I feel incredibly blessed to have found love again and to share life with him.

Since I had stayed home for so many years with my first four children, I assumed that would be the right thing to do with Lincoln. I loved spending the days with my sweet chubby baby, but I missed the aesthetic industry and yearned to get back into it. My sister, Andrea, encouraged me, over and over, to branch out on my own. I fearfully put together a business plan and grew cautiously optimistic. I opened Vibrant Med Spa in September 2015. I had everything set and announced I was ready to take clients. On my first day, I dropped all the kids off at school and immediately crawled back into bed, certain nobody had scheduled. As I lay in my cozy bed I thought I better log into my schedule to see if anyone had, and to my surprise, not one, but four people had scheduled with me. It was a Christmas miracle. I hopped out of bed, already dressed in my scrubs, and headed to work.

That first year I rented a one-room suite and it was the perfect way for me to start. It felt like a leap, but not too big for my britches. The second year I moved around the corner and rented two rooms. I also brought on board my first employee. By year three I was able to purchase my own business condo and expand even more. We are now into our sixth year and I feel so blessed to thrive, even with the shutdown of Covid-19.

I'm sharing the details of the last fifteen years of my life because I want you to know that if I can do it, you can do it. I am someone who wants things to be perfect, and nothing ever is. The action I challenge you to do is to be crystal clear on your why. What is driving you? Why do you want to get out of bed each day? Why do you want to work so hard for something? It makes it that much easier to push through the hard times when you know your why. Like I mentioned earlier, my children are my why. I want them to know that they can rise above any mistake or hardship if they're willing to give it their all. I want them to know that their mom would do anything for them to better their lives.

Give Others Grace

Getting back to finding myself through all of this, I think it's safe to say that I am an emotional creature. I feel things deeply and I love so hard. From any hurt I've felt as an adult or getting over childhood woes, I've come to know that connecting with my most authentic self is when I show someone the grace that I hope they're willing to show me. You also need to give yourself grace. Forgive yourself and do better.

Share Your Good Fortune with Others

I was always taught to pay a tithe, and I still practice this today. Not the exact same way I did in the past, but I do think the joy I feel in giving is worth every penny or service that I give away. I have been abundantly blessed in my times of need. I never want to forget my humble beginnings and so I'll continue to pay it forward.

Slow Down Enough to Notice the Beauty Around You

Connecting with your authentic self will look different for everyone. That's the beauty in our special individuality. My parents always pointed out the beauty on the earth and I'm forever grateful that I've been taught to slow down enough to notice these treasures. When my son Lincoln was four years old, I told him I had a surprise for him. I had just spotted a double rainbow out my back window and took him outside to see it. He placed his hand over his heart and exclaimed 'my God, that's a beautiful rainbow'! He asked if we could lay on the ground and look at it together. Does it get any more authentic than that? A tiny moment in my day to connect with my boy and with Mother Nature. Pause, breathe, and be grateful for that moment.

Busting Through Your Limiting Beliefs

I recommend therapy or hiring a coach to help you bust through your limiting beliefs. I have two people in my life right now who challenge me and cheer me on in just the right ways. Here's a valuable lesson I learned last week while talking to my business coach, Melissa Huetter. She asked me a question where I responded in a not so positive way, and she said 'Girl, that itty bitty shitty committee has got to go.' I laughed so hard, as I'd never heard that before, and I realised she was right. We're screaming the loudest at ourselves and we really need to do better at saying look at you go! Look at the improvement! You've got this!

My spiritual life coach, Dr Katie Henry, has given me a couple of great tools. The first is, when you're doubting something, simply put your hand on your heart, take a deep breath and ask if it's true. Does this feel right to you? For me, feeling and knowing go hand in hand. Trust your intuition. This is a gift we're all given. The other pearl I got from her was when she told me I was meant to be real, not perfect. I have this written on a board in my home to remind myself every day.

Just keep climbing. Keep pushing through the fear. We're all surviving, but it feels so much better to thrive.

Practice Gratitude

Remember to always practice gratitude. If you're in a dark mindset, you can still push yourself to find something to be grateful for. Maybe it's the blanket you're under that protects and comforts you. Maybe it's the microwave you have to warm up your take-out food. Something I'm grateful for every single day is the hug and kiss I get from my husband as he lovingly brushes my cheek. That small action fills me up and makes me feel so loved.

Our minds are mighty, and we get to pick if we're going to stay in a negative space or find something to be grateful for.

Show and Share Your Love with Others

The thing that feels most authentic to me is to love. Tell the people around you what they mean to you. Tell the woman struggling with her small toddler that she's doing a great job. Hug people. Smile at them. Notice what happens in your body when you do this. The energy is different, almost like something is humming inside.

You don't have to be perfect and it's important to recognise your growth along the way. When we act in a place of love and gratitude you will be amazed at the light and joy you can spread. It's infectious and you feel euphoric.

Find Out What Makes You Feel Most Authentic

I invite you to ask yourself what makes you feel connected to your most authentic self. I've shared a snippet of my story, and I hope it helps you realise that there's joy in the journey.

Blessings can come out of mistakes. Be intentional with your actions after making that mistake. Always seek truth, keep learning new ways to connect each day, and don't forget the power behind your smile.

Heidi Arambula

Heidi's professional career started later than most. She became a mother at the young age of twenty-one and found so much joy in staying home with her children.

After twelve years of marriage, she went through a major life shift when her marriage unexpectedly fell apart and she left the church she had been a devout member of her whole life.

Having no formal education, this was a scary time as the reality of needing to find a way to support her family became an instant need.

Heidi had always loved the beauty and wellness industry. She grew up making homemade skincare products and pampering her friends and family with her 'magic touch' massages, so she decided to go to laser aesthetic school.

She has now been in the medical aesthetic field for twelve years and is the founder/owner of Vibrant Med Spa in Round Rock, Texas.

Her vision is one that is constantly progressing, but her main goal is to help women feel comfortable in their own skin. It's not about altering your beauty, but rather giving you the confidence to age gracefully. She likes to promote the idea of pro-aging rather than anti-aging. She knows that beauty and wisdom come through experiences and should be celebrated.

Heidi knows firsthand that life doesn't always go the way we plan, but she believes when we lean into the pain and face the fear, there is beauty in the journey. When you do the hard work, you'll heal, you'll grow and you'll have the wisdom to help others.

Website: www.vibrantmedspa.com
Instagram: @www.instagram.com/vibrantmedspa
TikTok: @vibrantmedspa

DECODE YOUR PERSONAL POWER

INTRODUCTION

Tracey Jewel

Reclaim your worth, don't you dare
shrink for someone else's glory.
– Nikki Rowe

Marianne Williamson's quote about our light frightening us more than our darkness is something that I have always felt deeply.

> Our deepest fear is that we are powerful beyond measure. It is our light, not our darkness, that most frightens us. We ask ourselves, Who am I to be brilliant, gorgeous, talented, fabulous? Actually, who are you not to be? You are a child of God. Your playing small doesn't serve the world.

After working with an amazing Beautiful You life coach, Marlous Teh, I began to understand how much power I was giving away. Marlous took me through a process of realisation that I was like an energy grid. Not only was I letting others plug into my power (no boundaries), but I, too, was plugging into others, caring about what they thought and people pleasing.Unhooking from it all was the key to cutting cords, and developing clear and healthy boundaries before plugging back, and enabled me to decode my personal power.

Connecting to a higher power (of your choosing) I found was also a powerful way to boost my overall vibration. I have shared my anxiety story very publicly over the past few years. A lot of this anxiety came from a feeling of losing control, giving this control over to others and at the same time feeling like I had to do everything myself. One of the most important parts I learnt about connecting to some sort of higher power is feeling like you're protected and not alone. It helps you get into a different realm, and it helps you ground.

How to Up Your Personal Power

Personal power can manifest physically, before we feel it emotionally, mentally and spiritually. In the chapters that follow we will explore all aspects of personal power, but let's begin with the physical and the most basic symbol of power: posture. Start with a good, straight posture that indicates feelings of confidence and self-control. Physiology informs psychology, so you're actually more likely to feel happier when you sit up straight. When you are slumped down in a chair, however, you feel less powerful and more troubled.

But learning to take on a power pose doesn't just make you more confident, it actually changes your hormone levels and increases your propensity to take risks (Carney, Cuddy and Yap, 2010). Powerful poses usually consist of making the body bigger and taking up more space. Placing the hands on your hips, standing up taller, planting your feet firmly into the ground and even putting on a pair of high heels can instantly change how you feel.

And if there's one thing you take away from this article, it is to *never* cross your arms. Not only do people assume you're less credible, but it also tells people that you're closed off and unopen to new ideas or opinions. This posture can also indicate that you're uncomfortable with your size or weight, since we unconsciously try to cover the things we believe aren't 'good enough'. (Before I got my teeth straightened, I would always put my hand over my mouth when I laughed.)

Crossed legs tell a similar story. People will often stand with one leg crossed in front of the other when they're with a group of people they don't know well.

Tony Robbins speaks in all his events about physical state and changing your physiology if you want to change your life. When we start to change our physical states, emotions and mindset can radically shift.

BECOMING YOUR MOST POWERFUL SELF

Michelle Patrick

Power

It's an interesting word isn't it? From an early age, as we learn the miracle of speech, we begin the process of accepting words into our vocabulary that best suit the intellect of the world around us. We then identify with the learnt definitions of those words from a perspective of the acceptance of the word in our social constructs rather than its actual etymology. These two things can be extremely different. With that said, power can definitely feel like a dirty word due to the impact and use of it (sometimes negative and often abused) on our environments.

In the etymology of the word power, going back to its earliest origins, is 'Ability; ability to act or do; strength, vigour or might.'

Let's take these earlier origins and use them to explore our unique paths in our individual realities that pertain to being human.

Who are you?

We essentially are a melange of the learnt behaviours, socially correct norms and domesticated views passed down by our parents and their parents. We are little balls of malleable putty, often being moulded at will by the bioenergetics of existence. But what does it feel like to truly exist? What does it feel like to exist in a way that is entirely unique to your individual puzzle piece of consciousness? We are, after all, just a fractal of consciousness expressing itself uniquely through our individual journey. And as humans, we have learnt to trust the intellect of the 'word', rather than the intellect of consciousness, of creation.

When exploring the realms of personal power, we must first connect with our puzzle piece of the whole. Being human can be quite something. We are catapulted though life so fast that sometimes we can barely catch our breath, let alone take time to actually, and I mean actually, explore our piece of the puzzle – our curves, edges and texture. No two pieces of a puzzle are the same, and there would not be the completed image of the puzzle without all pieces. You are a puzzle piece to the geometry of life. You are tantra illuminated. You are a living, breathing and walking universe of your very own. You are miraculous and whole. There is nothing lacking in your ecology. You are frequently just burdened with layers of self-doubt, self-worth issues, and conditions and expectations of a world that does everything but help actualise your unique fingerprint on the world. That would be stepping into personal power, and to know where you're going, you must know where you've come from. That would be inviting the universe to bend to your will. That would be sitting in the driver's seat of this amazing piece of engineering called the body, and adventuring with all the possibilities of you. And you are definitely possible.

It took me quite a while to step into what I would consider my personal power. From a very young age, I was extremely confused about who I was. I never really fitted in anywhere. Most of all, I had a deep inner knowing that I may not want to. Sure, I wanted to feel into the collective consciousness of a tribe, but I didn't want to follow one. And when I did, I was anxious, depressed and frankly uninspired. I always felt there was more for me than the black and white reality of having my cloth cut the same shape as others. We are all cut from the same cloth, but no two shapes are the same. They can't be. Until around the age of seventeen, this was something I struggled with deeply and daily.

I have always had a deep affinity to the realities of alternative medicine. It was honestly a calling from a very young age. I used to roll around the fields in the villages I grew up in. Early on I developed a profound inquisitiveness for the natural world, having an immeasurable knowing that somehow we were more connected to it than simply using it for pleasurable viewing and the inevitable exchange of oxygen and carbon dioxide. Even that exchange blew my young mind. It was a sure sign of the symbiotic fusion shared between the human form and the natural world. I'm speaking of a bioenergetic exchange that extends beyond the rose tinted and shorted sighted glasses of human vision.

So, it was at seventeen, when I became seriously entrenched in my studies, both formal and holistically, that I began expanding into the wisdom and intellect of consciousness and creation, from ancient to contemporary. Whether naturopathy, herbal or Chinese medicine, different spiritualities, or Daoist studies, these systems, though all unique in their revelation, all had a thread that was of distinct interest to me. I was deeply drawn to our symbiotic relationship to nature and our ability though expansion, discipline and awareness to take control of our internal environments and harness personal power.

Let's explore some ideals of personal power from a bioenergetic view, using our innate energy centres as a foundation.

Let's start by examining the solar plexus. This energy centre, our third chakra (or Manipura in Sanskrit), is actively mobilised when we assert ourselves in the world. This centre, when rooted in its essence, gives us the potent ability to radiate our personal power into the world. Its characteristics are that of a pure, unadulterated will, personal power, and mental ability and agility. Most of us have energetic blocks and imbalances, as well as energy-sabotaging habitual behaviours, that inhibit us from fully accessing our capacity in full vitality. This can lead to us feeling exhausted, scattered, dull and even ill. When the solar plexus chakra is in full bloom, and the energy of this centre is in full equilibrium, there are multiple personal qualities that can be harvested. We are able to take responsibility for our life. Our mental ability becomes vibrant and the intellect becomes spacious. We are able to form clear personal options (yes, you are allowed those) and beliefs. Our decision making becomes clear and our vision allows us to see and set clear direction. This is where the clarity of judgment forms. You will align clearly with your personal identity and express your unique personality, at will, with self-assurance and confidence. Most importantly, through self-discipline, a wild independence is found. When the energy in this centre is in balance, these attributes function with clarity, grace and ease.

However, when blocked or overactive, you will experience symptoms and pathologies ranging from energetic to emotional and also physical. The very word Manipura translates to 'City of Jewels'. Therefore, you can see from its very meaning what we can find within ourselves from stepping into this energy. You see, nothing is ever separate. We are a complete living mandala. When we experience challenges in our emotional, mental or physical health (through colonised ideas of wellness), we find ourselves frantically grappling to elevate the symptom that manifests, rather than working from the very soils of ourselves to bring homeostasis to our whole existence. So, when vison and clarity in direction is lacking, depleting your ability to initiate personal power, it is here that one must be willing to explore the very essence of 'why'. It is here your answers and prescription will be found. This is the way of activating your inner physician.

Personal power is essentially the harvest from the state of your internal environment. The organs associated with this energy centre are the stomach and the spleen. In the foundations of the ancient philosophy of five element theory, these organs are representative of the earth element within us, which is represented by the season of late summer and the harvesting of crops. Within this philosophy, imbalance within our internal organs can cause emotional pathology, which can then lead to mental disturbance. In the spirit of symbiosis, we can see how the frequency of this enactment does the honourable thing and returns this discomfort back to the organ. And there you have it, not only is your physical health having a blowout, but your emotional and mental stability is now walking out the door with it … with you watching it leave with no real understanding of why.

Again, I reiterate, you are whole.

You are a whole universe. You are a walking mind and everything inside of you is woven like a fine Persian rug. So when questioning chronic imbalance in your personal attributes, it is vital to enter self-observation and radical self-responsibility, to understand your internal terrains. That's personal power. The cultivation of this very subject exists not only in the energetic centres discussed, but in the organs that inhabit it. You can do all the journaling for personal power you like, yet if your spleen and stomach Qi is weak, it's like fishing with no bait.

You see, there is no quick way to cultivate personal power. I know that's probably not what you want to hear, but there isn't. It definitely takes a journey for the tides to cross the ocean before they meet the shore, generating power and strength as they meet the rising ocean floor. We are all doing the best we can 'humaning'. I get it. It's tough. And what makes is tougher, is that we have been conditioned out of the virtue of patience and into one of convenience. Yet, it has taken a lifetime for you to get here, to be reading this chapter right now. And the fact you are reading this collaboration, shows an interest in self-awareness, improvement and observation.

If personal power is something you wish to cultivate, as you should, then self-observation within this amazing piece of engineering we call the body, is where the seeds are sown, watered, weeded and harvested. Speaking back of the spleen and stomach as a potential point of weakness along with the solar plexus, are you aware that the stomach and spleen are directly linked to the mind? I'm sure you are. You have at some point experienced the uncomfortable sensations of feeling worried and/or concerned about something, and feeling it directly in your gut. But worry and persistent anxious thinking about unpleasant things can also be a pathology of deficiency in the energy of the stomach and spleen. This is going to inhibit your ability to cultivate personal power because the vibrational essence of the physical matter involved is weak. These organs that digest our food and distribute the nutrients through our bodies, create the energy we need to do what we do in the world. On a psychological level, this process enables us to digest our experiences and impressions and turn them into usable ideas and concepts. In a healthy state, we readily absorb the impressions that we need for psychological growth and development, and we let go of those that are not useful so that we do not take on concepts that do not belong to us. We have a clear sense of what and how much we need to grow. If there is a constitutional weakness of the spleen causing a habitual response to excess stress and insufficient life support, worry can be part of a self-perpetuating and vicious cycle. The more energy we expend in this useless mental activity, the less we have available to nourish our body, mind and solar plexus and to take steps to create the life we really want to live. If the mind and body are weak as a result of this deficiency, we have less and less capacity to move forward on our life path and manifest our highest and truest purpose – our personal power and the mandate of our destiny.

So what? You may have a stomach and spleen deficiency. Your solar plexus may be a little shot from just doing life and doing life in a way that does not foster your unique conscious imprint in the world. But it's all recoverable.

You are the driver of your spaceship for life. You are your own commander.

A miracle manifests. And therefore, you are the creator of miracles. Personal power is not something you learn. Yes, we can learn the vocabulary of it, but it is something that arises from within. It is already given. However, expanding into your holistic being will activate the physical, emotional and spiritual remembrance of this. I invite you to go forth. Explore what brings your solar plexus into balance. Go and nourish your spleen and then harvest all that personal power. Remember, it's the journey. None of us have yet reached our final destination.

It gets to be so beautiful.

You already are.

Michelle Patrick

Michelle Patrick is a clinically experienced doctor of Chinese medicine and naturopathic nutrition, with an invested passion and interest in self-mastery and five element theory and philosophy.

Michelle believes that the human body is capable of great self-healing and expansion when the physical, emotional and spiritual bodies align in their divine thread of consciousness – when you are in the sovereign state of your own wellness and in the integrity of embodiment.

Through her dedicated practice, Michelle supports the awakening of this capability in her patients and clients – by not only supporting them with the application of treatment, but providing them with a framework that supports the holistic person, allowing the body and its subtle bodies to ignite homeostasis.

Website: www.themichellepatrick.com
Email: Michelle@themichellepatrick.com

NINE SECRETS FOR STAYING IN YOUR PERSONAL POWER

Annamaya Ananda

God's GIFT to you is the WISDOM gained through travelling along the tunnel of the light and tunnel of the dark.
– Annamaya

As an ambitious, talented over-achiever, I spent all my twenties excelling at sport, at university and in my career. I had the golden touch on everything I wanted to have, do and be. Things I wanted, I almost always got. Somehow, I got coded with an encryption for a determined mind and courageous heart, as I have always been brave enough to fully embrace everything I set my mind on.

I am sure an insatiable drive and self-motivation got awakened in me from a young age. My dad had me listening to Zig Ziglar from my earliest years, as well as posting motivational quotes around my bedroom walls. Our school motto was even 'girls can do anything'. But it took me years to discover that my tenacity and drive are what have allowed me to hold things together: a stoic fierceness to stay on course, to stay committed to my goals no matter what I am faced with. However, I would not be authentic in my word if I said it was the path of least resistance. So much of what I have overcome or achieved has not come easily or without incessant challenges.

In October 2013, at thirty-three, I was diagnosed with an autoimmune disease called hypothyroidism. Within a week I had told my employer, and I also found out I was three months pregnant with our second son. Whilst on sick leave, and the night before going to Bali on our first family holiday in almost two years, I was 'let go' by way of redundancy over the phone. My employer said to me 'how can you do your job if pregnant?' That turned into being unexpectedly unemployed, unemployable and a long five-month 'unfair dismissal' fair work case, that was settled only one month before my son was born, in March 2014.

By April 2014, a further diagnosis came: Hashimoto's, along with adrenal fatigue. As a result, I was bedridden eighteen hours a day with my newborn for the rest of 2014. By June 2014, my kids' father and I separated so I had a three-month-old and four-year-old who I struggled day to day to care for. So much for that 'forever man' being by my side to protect, support and care for me during my bad times (he was completely unsupportive and hurtful along the way).

If 2014 wasn't bad enough, 2015 saw me go from bad to worse, in every possible way and in every area of my life.

Come January 2015, I realised during my first kundalini experience that despite all my efforts to try and heal my relationship, it wasn't working; all I could now focus on was me and my healing journey. For whatever path I was going to take, I was now not prepared to ignore my emotions, put anything under the carpet, suppress my pain and my power or dim my light for anyone any longer.

Late February, a further blow came, this time from my father (the man I cherished and saw as the hero and rock in my life). By phone, he shared with me an ultimatum my stepmother had given him; he was being forced, backed into a corner, to openly choose between her or me. Choosing her was enraging for me. It was devastating to hear the hurtful words of the sudden abandonment from the man who had centred his world and lifetime around his two daughters (raising us on his own from six years of age) and who had such a strong, close connection to me, and to discover he could so easily walk away because of the insecurities of his wife.

By late March 2015, a series of mystical events happened after a full moon ceremony and past life regression session (where I realised I had no memories at all before the age of twelve and felt like my internal computer hard drive had permanently deleted those 'under twelve' files). The universe had a plan for me to understand these years, to unpack the forgotten trauma and pain.

God delivered to me, out of nowhere, three significant women (individually coming to me) from my childhood to fill in my 'memory gap' over the following two weeks. This set off a nervous breakdown. I cried uncontrollably, for I had no idea of what my life really was or what to believe or not believe, as so much that was shared conflicted with what I thought I knew.

By now my kids' father had temporarily moved back in. This time he was even more emotionally and mentally abusive, hurtful, cruel and unsupportive than ever before. How could I have partnered with a man who was emotionless and lacked any sense of compassion or concern for my wellbeing – yelling and abusing me, and unable to sit and hold me or just let me know he was there for me.

I knew I was now in a challenging situation, but I had no way of knowing what to do. All I felt was fear. I was completely alone and helpless in a world where I didn't feel wanted, protected or supported by anyone – the 'rejected one'. Even while being in a relationship and having 'all' the things – home, investments, cash in the bank, kids, partner – it did not feel like a dream life. It was more a nightmare I was waking up to each day, and I was not willing to stand for abuse, cruelty or emotional blackmail anymore.

Six weeks later, during a workshop, I was allowed for the first time in my life to cry out all the pain I remembered from my life. It was where I also came across, by two-way transmission and direct communication, a spiritual guru from India. In a place I didn't know – a place of complete non-judgement, I released a lifetime of pain, a life full of my own fears: fear of rejection and abandonment, of feeling unworthy and unlovable, and a fear of not being able to be me. It was in this moment, I chose to declare the very things I wanted for my life.

Finally, I found a path and was able to start truly healing my wounds. Yet, to help those declarations be realised, I had to first lose everything I had built my life on: people, loved ones, family and illusions.

I had to learn to rebuild the foundations of my future self from these new truths – truths of who I truly am, who I want to be, what I want for my life and what I hold most dear to me.

Following that spiritual path with the spiritual guru from India for over four years, was the sole reason I have come out as I am. The path was able to make sense of the chaos and to help explain my inner and outer turmoil. I truly chose to learn and embrace how this ancient wisdom from the east could give me the context and understanding of how to live my most powerful self in the modern world with modern challenges.

This path, without a single doubt, was my biggest teacher. Upon reflection, many years later and after many tears cried out in pain, I can now bring complete forgiveness to my heart and soul for not knowing a better path, a path that could have been pain free, and not knowing how I could have done things differently. At the same time, I can love myself for choosing a path most would follow when going headfirst into battle and to stand up for what mattered to me: my children.

In hindsight 2014–2018 truly tested me in every way imaginable, including have to cope with a very long, drawn-out and traumatic custody battle, where I was made to defend my sanity and my ability to parent and to challenge the many ludicrous, outlandish, irrational and blatant lies said in court by the father of my kids. He persisted in refusing me rights to my children or the right for me to choose how to parent. Initially, he wanted me to have only three hours supervised visits a fortnight based on zero evidence for such a claim.

I was forced to take the stand in court and to stand up for me, my ability to parent and my sanity (a day I dreaded and which made my stomach churn for months beforehand). Yet God had better plans for me. I needed that day on the stand more than I realised. What erupted that day on the stand was my power to defend myself and stand authentically for me, despite the eyes of hate against me. I truly believe now that it is not until you are put in challenging situations, backed into a corner just trying to survive and breathe, that you realise your true power.

When you are tested beyond what you think is possible, you see your strength and your resilience. The pain persisted right till the end, when the judge said I was a perfectly good mother and that I was not inflicting any of my spiritual beliefs on my children or in any way negatively parenting my kids.

The amount of pain I endured from family, past friends and people who knew me, I never wish on anyone. I knew I would never end my own life, even though I could see how someone with no support and with no one to turn to, could easily make that decision.

My understanding of family and friends became so messed up because the idea of having loyal family and friends watching my back was not my reality. I had no one, and I mean no one at all, to turn to as authentically as me during those early painful years.

I had people I thought of as friends betray me, go against my agreements and help my former partner attempt to break into my home. Another allowed him to come into my home unannounced and go through it and take pictures of it to use against me in court. And the list keeps going on. It broke and violated every sense of trust, privacy and support I had in friends, loved ones, family and authority figures.

What was really hurtful, was never once was anyone answerable for their actions, behaviours, lies, betrayal, blackmail or manipulative tactics. I could not believe in the injustice of it all.

For years, during dark moments I would just lie under my doona, afraid and scared of the world and hoping the floor would open and something would come and take me away from it all so that I could escape the pain in my heart. I wanted to fall down a sinkhole and run away. That hole never came, but somehow I kept choosing the baby steps needed to keep consciously working on me.

Many people understandably numb their pain with an addiction or negative influence. In contrast to that, I chose to get healthy in every way – physically, mentally, emotionally, financially and spiritually – and to fully embrace how to find resilience within, how to strengthen my mind, body and soul through practising things like fasting, enemas, daily practice, spiritual routine, motivational mentors, mediation and coaching, to constantly unpack trauma and choose life. Yet through it all I was being made to feel like someone crazy, someone who should be in a 'mental institution' according to my kids' father's affidavit, to feel I should follow his thoughts on how I should live and not go against them. Yet I endured years of hurtful attacks on me. What was sad was all these people failed to see I was trying to sort myself and my life out so I could be a better mum and a healthy role model for my kids.

I never forced anyone to think or believe in what I did. I chose to focus living each day in a way that could help and heal me. And yet no one wanted to understand that actual truth.

I chose to stand authentically as me and in what I believed in every day, in the epicentre of a three-year, painful, daily, intense storm, no matter what was being projected at me, happening to me and being told of me and no matter what lies I was being accused of – knowing that justice and truth had to one day come out.

For *eight years* I endured the toughest time for my heart, the most painful experiences of my life.

I chose to heal my heart and heal my life, putting it back together piece by piece. I chose an intentional life – to love, to offer large amounts of service to others for many years, to take complete self-responsibility for my emotional state and help keep my mind free and focused towards my future visions.

I cried a lot during the months after that judgement, in gratitude to God for answering my prayers. Many years later, it still gets me teary-eyed thinking how I felt in that moment.

What I learned was to not find a way to escape the fires of life, but to find a way to stand in the fires and not get burned, to not be brought to my knees helpless and powerless, to learn to find a way to stand in the ring and be a fighter, to learn to find a way to not avoid the storm, but to be calm during the storm.

This is only some of my story. Thank you for being here with me along the way.

I am Annamaya.

I choose to be the nourisher of souls, helping them as they commit to uplevelling their life and looking for a way out of the chaos, mess and struggles they are in.

I am a passionate woman, who has activated a warrior heart, a thirst to want to nourish the souls around me, standing for a new way of being, a new way of living life powerfully no matter what life presents.

I am inspired to take a stand, as I see so many women all around me having lost their feminine power, the essence of who they truly are, their true magnetic self. Feminine personal power is the strongest essence from where we all originated. It is where life is drawn to you, where things come to you as your vibrational match, where dame spirit (the feminine of the king spirit) stands charismatically, energetically and powerfully in her warrior, grounded truth.

I believe in truly wanting to help share what worked for me. I feel so grateful to be able to share the practices that helped every part of my journey across every part of my life.

Annamaya's Nine Sacred Secrets to Staying in Your Personal Power

CONNECTION (to help you stay grounded)

Every single day, take some time to connect to the Divine (God, source, universe)

MEDITATION (to stay emotionally balanced)

Do this upon waking up and last thing before going to sleep.

SELF-TALK (to control and influence how you think and act)

Choose to be fully responsible for what you say to yourself.

What may help you: YouTube, podcasts, write a letter to your future self, journaling, time in nature, singing out loud, ecstatic dance to get into your body and out of your heart, and creative play just as a little child would.

EMOTIONAL AWARENESS (Accept and recognise ALL emotions are real and valid.)

Your intuition is your greatest guide. There are two approaches you can choose:

- READ THE ENERGY (What's REALLY going on?)
- Know what conversations to have (even if feeling vulnerable, uncertain, or scared).
- Know what conversations not to have.
- JOURNALING EXERCISE (In a quiet place, ask yourself what is really going on.)
- What am I feeling right now?
- Where am I feeling it in my body?
- When was the earliest memory of this feeling?
- What did I most need at the time?
- What was most missing in that moment?
- What did I most long for back then?
- How can I give this to myself right now?
- Now choose one of releasing rituals below to let it go.

STRENGTHEN YOUR NERVOUS SYSTEM (Increase your resilience.)

This will help you withstand life and any uncomfortable experiences.

- fasting and enemas (break emotional patterns stored in food)
- cryotherapy (cold therapy)
- oxygen therapy
- frequency therapy (super effective way to influence of energetic state).

REMOVE TOXICITY (Remove what is toxic to you.)

All negative energy is bad for you (emotional, mental, spiritual, physical). How:

- food (plant-based living food over chemical laden, processed 'dead' food)
- chemicals (in food, cleaning products, make-up and so on)
- water (Install a filter system in your home. Use high vibration water only.)
- people (Remove people who bring anger, rage, drama, abuse or toxic energy to you, anyone who makes you less of who you are.)
- spiritually (Remove things like mainstream media, porn and horror movies.)

UNPACK YOUR TRAUMA (Suffering is when you keep repeating painful experiences. This will liberate you of emotional triggers and stop you repeating painful cycles.)

Find a quiet place and journal out your responses to these questions:

- When you explore your body, where do you feel this in you?
- What belief or thought were you telling yourself during that experience? (That is: Why did they do it to me?)
- What is the opposite of this thought? What if this was not about me but about them?
- Is there any chance of that opposite thought being true?
- How has this strengthened me now?

TOP SIX VALUES IN YOUR WHEEL OF LIFE (Every 3–6 months determine what are the most important values across all areas of your life using the Wheel of Life.)

Your Wheel of Life is made of eight Areas of Life.

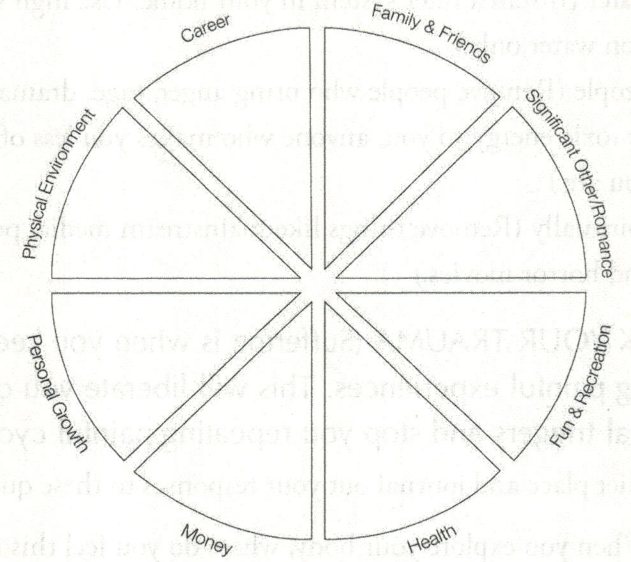

Step 1: WHEEL OF LIFE DIAGRAM

Using the blank wheel of life diagram, answer these questions for each of the eight areas (each pie of the circle) shown above:

- What are your top six values for this area?
- Example: For the Family and Friends Area of Life, the top six values could be connection, openness, trust, love, kindness and respect.
- Rank each of the six values from the top value (#1) to least high value (#6).

- Example: For the Family and Friends Area of Life, the top six values in order could be:
- unwavering love (has your back and expresses love)
- connection (close bond, support, vulnerable, judgement free)
- openness (willingness to share)
- trust (can confide in them)
- kindness (treat you with thought and care)
- respect (accepts you fully, despite choices, beliefs, opinions, lifestyle)
- Now complete this for each of the eight Areas of the Wheel of Life.

Step 2: INTEGRATION and EMBODIMENT (so that you live your life intentionally to your top values)

- What would life look like if you lived intentionally to your values?
- How would that happen or how would it not be happening?

Example: For the Health and Wellness Area of Life from the Wheel of Life –

- I will eat nourishing food.
- I will be checking in with what I say to myself when I make food choices.
- I will plan my week of food and meals so I don't get caught out or make bad choices when hungry.

RELEASING RITUALS (how to handover to God and let go)

- FIRE RITUAL: Write out on paper what you want to create, what you want to let go of, what you want to handover to. Now burn your papers and handover those desires to God.
- LOVE LETTER TO GOD: Write a letter that details your wishes to God.
- PRAYER: Say the ho'oponopono prayer.
- FORGIVENESS EXERCISE: Write a letter to the person you want to forgive, then burn it and hand over the rest to God.
- GRATITUDE: Each day write out ten reasons why you are grateful for the day

To awaken your power is not about some magic pill, potion or person. It is about addressing the core of who you are, what you stand for, where your passion lies and what the point of you being here in this world is. When you start to find clarity in these answers, a whole new awakening happens. Suddenly there's an inspired drive. You wake up ready to take on the world, and there's an energy, even magnetism, about you that you can't hide from. It just radiates from your very essence. There's a flow about you, a receptivity that has you drawing life to you not away from you, where you show up in your fullest, most authentic expression of who you truly are, the light and the shade. You own it all, and there you are with passion, purpose and influencing the world with your high energy and vitality.

In this chapter I have shared only a small snippet of what I have been through. So much has been left out. It is enough to share the last eight years of what I needed to find me – the real feminine power

I have always had in me but wouldn't dare express or embody. Who I am did not come easily or without resistance. I seemed to have always chosen the right path, not the easy path. And with that has come a lot of facing up to myself and others in ways that made me think at times I was crazy for putting myself through these rings of fire. But part of me also knew I am not here to dim my light for anyone else anymore. I am here to shine my genius and show you how to step into and stay in your personal power as you uplevel your life.

Next Steps

In my life I had to let go of foundations built on the illusions of pain, trauma, abandonment and chaos, and to realise that nothing of my past painful experiences was here to cause me to fall short of who I truly am. I have been given each of these opportunities, as chaotic and at times unbearably painful as they were, as a catalyst and means for me to find myself and my personal power and to awaken my magic and gifts to the world.

On my journey of finding who I truly am, I have found many women who have lost their way, their power and who they truly are, just like I had. If you are like I was, this is the right place for your personal transformation.

My promise to you is to give you the tools and the top resources you can use to step into and stay in your personal power, no matter what life throws at you.

My desire is to truly help you stay in your personal power as you uplevel your life – whether that be your personal or business life. Both are intrinsically connected and I'm here to help you uplevel to the version of you waiting on the other side of my coaching containers.

I provide womb-like, safe containers, using a combination of coaching containers and frequency therapy, to awaken the dormant yet powerful life force within you, so you can live a life of freedom, joy and liberation.

Your personal power means showing up in life knowing you can withstand anything personally or professionally.

xox

Much love and power from 'The Soul Nourisher', recognised globally as 'Annamaya'.

I love connecting with others. Reach out through my website www.iamannamaya.com or any of my social media platforms. I can support you in your personal or business quest so that you can learn to step into and stay in your personal power as life happens for you.

So please know this from
my SOULFUL heart to yours …
(beautiful radiant woman reading this passage)
You are Thine and YOUR SOUL is pure MAGIC. Time to
SPRINKLE your MAGIC on the world.
– Annamaya

Annamaya Ananda

Have you let life get the better of you?

Have you found yourself in a world of chaos?

Have you allowed setbacks or negative experiences to influence your mood and how you show up to the world?

If you said yes to any of these (I had said yes to all three questions), then I know that life is or has been troubling you in some way.

You don't wake up one day and realise you have power and resilience. In my case, time and time again I was backed into a corner and forced to take a stand, forced to stand up for me or those who had no voice to speak up. No matter how deeply I felt I was sinking into the quicksand of life through the constant battles of manipulation, abuse, blame, shame, loss, grief and greed, I was not prepared to be a bystander, sitting on the side-lines of my life. I have put myself into the fire, into the ring of life, and stood facing head-on the challenges others were not willing to deal with, as I met up against their traumas, unresolved issues and lack of self-responsibility. When I remember how many dark nights I endured, left helpless and without anyone to care for me, left lonely and isolated by a world I thought didn't want me or care for me, I sometimes feel overwhelmed.

In the end I chose to find me, to heal my heart, to choose each day to spread love and light on the world.

I now stand in my personal power through the embodiment and empowerment of my choices, beliefs and values.

Together, let's rise and become the greatest expression of who we each truly are, and let's go live the life we are truly here for. We are not here to suffer forever, play small or miss out on living the best life possible.

xoxox

Much love to you. May the world you live in be impacted by your brilliance and radiance.

Love and light from the 'The Soul Nourisher' known more widely as 'Annamaya'.

Qualifications:

- MBA (sustainability and management major), commerce, business (major in human resources), photography (six years with major in fine arts), results coaching, Presenting Like a Pro, NLP, professional writing, retail operations. Life Bliss University, Bangalore India (10+ spiritual programs).

Achievements:

- Selected for Victorian and Australian inline hockey and ice hockey teams (1994–2014).
- Formerly in the corporate sector and now business owner (20+ years) – national sales, multi state manager, start-up general manager for Bounceinc (20+ countries globally), general manager of not-for-profit organisation (supporting Down's syndrome) and key selected team member of projects that brought innovation, talent and new industry to markets here and overseas.
- Multi-award recipient in sports and business.

- Host of more than fifty workshops and events on mindset, business, business strategy, vision and resilience.
- Coaching locally and internationally (individuals, teams and organisations) for success in business and or in life.
- International business consultant, mentor, multi-business owner, facilitator, host, speaker, coach at workshops and events, Interview Series host (series 2 and 3 are now live), creator of the 'Global Frequency Movement' and 'Global Frequency Collective' online communities bringing the power of frequencies to global audiences.
- For those curious as to the meaning of my name, Annamaya Ananda, it means: Nourishing from the source of life, always in the highest state of consciousness and radiating the ultimate state of bliss.

How you and Annamaya can work together:

- One-on-one immersion coaching experience (with limited number of clients a year)
- Partner with Annamaya in one of her businesses.
- She is sharing the next evolution in holistic health and financial freedom via frequency therapy.
- She is sharing the next evolution of financial freedom and financial impact through passive income initiatives that she is aligned with.
- By request or invitation, Annamaya can be available for group coaching, facilitating, hosting and speaking at workshops, events (online or in person).

What she is currently working on:

Annamaya is a transformation coach using frequency therapy and business partnerships to help people as they uplevel across the following areas of their life: emotional, mental, physical, spiritual, and financial.

How you can work with Annamaya:

Every year Annamaya works with a select group of private clients. If you are truly committed to change and can invest time and dedication, you may be suited to this exclusive approach.

Her main focus is offering you an opportunity to partner with her across one of her businesses, where she includes coaching as part of those containers.

She opens invitations to be part of your events locally and overseas. These requests to be emailed to her at ma.annamaya@gmail.com.

Website: http://www.iamannamaya.com/

Facebook: https://www.facebook.com/annamaya.ananda/

Instagram: https://www.instagram.com/iamannamaya/

Email: hello@iamannamaya.com

CREATING MIRACLES

The magic of rapid, positive, lasting change

Dr Joy Martina &
Dr Roy Martina

Courage when you are scared is tapping into the powerful you that you are.

During a seminar, a man named Hans volunteered to come on stage. He had shoulder problems and couldn't raise his arm above his shoulder.

'I tore my ligaments twelve years ago in a ski accident,' he said. 'I've had three surgeries and am taking pain medication. Do you think your magic will work on me?'

I smiled and said, 'Magic is only magic if we cannot explain it! A better question is, is your heart open to receiving miracles? Do you believe you are worthy of a miracle? Or are you saying "No" to the impossible in your mind and want to stay where you are? Did you come on stage to prove you are an impossible case?'

He looked shocked and started to say, 'But…'

I stopped him. 'Let's make it easy,' I said. 'Do you want to be healed, and do you give yourself permission to experience something you cannot understand? Or do you want to resist a miracle because you enjoy being a victim and getting attention for your story?'

After a pause, I decided to further simplify the options. '"Yes" means you want a miracle. "No" means you want to waste my time. Please decide,' I said.

Of course, he said 'Yes', and ten minutes later he was pain-free and could move his arm like the accident never happened. That day, Hans's life changed, and he followed all our workshops to become a trainer in Switzerland. In three years, he stopped smoking, lost twenty-five kilos and helped hundreds of clients experience miracles like he had experienced on stage.

The Mindset for Miracles

There are two ways to experience miracles: the first is an unconscious process. It happens to you; maybe you didn't even expect it and you certainly cannot explain it.

The second is that miracles happen frequently in your life and you appear to be lucky. There may be different ways to get there, but it's always about stretching your mind beyond the realm of logical thinking. To the outside world, you are a magician. Some may believe you're a witch, or an airy-fairy person who believes in angels, symbols, mantras, meditation and quantum jumping, or a dreamer who makes vision boards hoping that one day the images on their collage will magically manifest in their life. Some will discuss the realm of quantum physics with you and how to best use the power of intention, visualisations, lowering your brainwaves to theta and then elevating them to gamma waves with elevated emotions of bliss, gratitude, happiness and visions of your future.

1. Forgetting what you know is bliss. Step one is to forget what you know and realise that all you've learnt comes from the blind teaching the blind how to give meaning to what they observe without a functional visual system. The blind believe that what they perceive is all there is. But you perceive less than 4 per cent of reality.

2. New skillsets. We unconsciously create 90 per cent of reality, trapping us in our own Mental Prison.

To escape, we need to learn the following skillsets:

- To use our intention as a tool of creation.
- To lower our brainwaves to theta (deep relaxation) to completely bypass our thinking mind and go into the field where we know nothing and can never know more than 1 per cent (no matter how much time we spend in that field). That is why we need our intention, so we know what information we want to access in the field of infinite possibilities; knowing that all information in this field is in waveform or just frequency.
- To allow the magic to happen, we need to keep removing any attachment to the outcome and any expectation or desire to force the result.
- To relax and keep alignment with the infinite field of possibilities and learn how it communicates with us; to direct us to be in the right place at the right time for the magic to happen. Miracles happen most often when you least expect them.

Summary: Intent-Relax and Allow. Each step is important. When Hans came on stage, we helped him get clear on his intent by removing his excuses as to why a miracle was impossible. That relaxed his brainwaves and he was de-hypnotised from his beliefs when we did not buy into his excuses and opened his mind to the infinite possibilities of the quantum information field, which has many names: the universe, morphogenetic field, God, higher self, five-dimensional realm, and so on. Pick whichever name you like, just don't believe you know how it works. This type of magic you do not control, you cannot force it, you just align with it.

Think of two tuning forks. When they have the same frequency (alignment), the one vibrating highest will move the second one into alignment. The intention is the alignment with the blueprint of what you want. Then you have to lower your brainwaves to get out of your overthinking, over-rationalising, busy head and allow your heart to open to feel deserving of health, wealth, healing, happiness and all you desire. You must pay attention to any background noise coming from your beliefs, past experiences and teachings from your blind educators.

Why is bad good?

I'll never forget a conversation I had with a student almost forty-five years ago. At the time, Robbie was a seventeen-year-old martial arts student and I was his sensei (teacher). After his first tournament, he came to me at a crossroads. During his first fight, he was hit on the liver and badly injured two ribs. He came to me crying, his ego completely destroyed, and in his embarrassment and frustration was ready to quit fighting forever.

I whispered in his ear, 'I am so happy that this happened!'

He stopped crying and, in shock, looked at me and asked, 'What do you mean, why are you happy for my loss?'

I smiled and said, 'The decision you make today will decide if you become a world champion or a loser for the rest of your life. A world champion learns from his mistakes. A loser believes that he is a loser and does not learn that every loss shows you what you have to improve. If you had won, you would have learnt nothing and would have become arrogant and then sooner or later you would lose without having learnt this lesson. The only difference is that your arrogance would have become your downfall! You are a champion – start behaving like one!'

Then I walked away. Robbie Kaman became a kickboxing world champion and was called 'The Living Legend!' We are still friends after forty years.

Why did that change his destiny? The truth is, I changed the meaning he gave to his loss. When we give meaning to an incident, the associated belief can stick with us for life. If you see your traumas as potential seeds for growth, you are developing the mindset for miracles. It's not about optimism, it's about the meaning you give to an experience. If the meaning opens doors to learning, better awareness, and transforming your perception, you will be more aligned with the impossible than when you accept defeat or complain about the difficulty of the challenge.

Your new mantra must be: 'All that happens that challenges me is my opportunity to grow stronger and wiser!' Or, as one of our students loves to say: 'In the end, all will be great. If it isn't great now, it isn't the end!'

Daydreaming: The last secret ingredient of the magic sauce

Most people have vague goals: a partner that is kind and loving, a big house or more houses, health, financial freedom, and so on. All of those dreams are confirming one thing: what you don't have. That creates separation between where you are and where you want to go. It increases the feeling of lack.

Every hour of the day, your feelings determine the spectrum of information that you are beaming into the universe. Like a tuning fork, you are sending out packets of information. The universe needs to adapt to those frequencies and, as a result, you receive more things that will resonate with the frequencies you are sending out. In other words, if you feel bad, miserable, sick or down regularly, that will override all the other frequencies you are sending out. If you envision a future in which you are the happiest, healthiest, most successful person you can be while making a difference for the planet, which gives you that happy, satisfied feeling that you are doing something that has no other gain than feeling good, you are resonating with higher frequencies.

The formula

Feelings are the carrier waves of the information of what you want. And the universe has no choice other than to align itself with those frequencies and bring you what matches those frequencies. Daydreaming means spending time with that future where you experience these elevated emotions. That will create a shift towards that future. There are three factors:

- the intensity of the elevated emotions
- the time you spend in these elevated moods (Short bursts of high intensity are better than long periods of time in less intense feelings.)
- How relaxed your brainwaves are.
- Your brainwaves should be relaxed, which is why daydreaming is better than intense focus. The best times are when

you are just waking up, in the afternoon after lunch (take a small recess) and when you are ready to fall asleep.

How to become a Miracle Worker

1. Start your morning daydreaming about the future.

Lose yourself in the feelings of gratitude for the opportunities that are coming: gratitude for more time to make a difference and contribute to a better world, connecting with all the happy people you will affect in the future and resonating with their feelings of gratitude for your contributions.

2. Set your intention for the day.

How do you want to feel at the end of the day when you look back? What do you want to create today? How do you want the people to feel who cross your path? Visualise the outcome while riding the waves of the daydreaming phase you are still in.

3. Notice when you aren't in alignment with elevated emotions.

Anytime you feel distracted by emotions, stress, triggers, beliefs, or thoughts that lower your frequencies, do a pattern interrupt. Try breathing, walking, music, or asking yourself questions like 'How can I change my state now?' Do whatever it takes to elevate your emotional state to happiness, contentment, curiosity, bliss, and so on.

4. Take a sacred time out.

When possible, fit in a twenty-minute break where you are not distracted by your phone, people, weather or noise. Close your eyes and daydream about your future and connect with the elevated feelings of that future. Imagine being your Future Self and projecting all the resources you need into your Future Self. Then imagine resonating with and having those resources.

5. Bedtime.

Before sleep, evaluate your day and scan for moments where you lost alignment and imagine doing those scenes over again, but now in your power of connection to your Future Self. Visualise what you would do differently if you were your Future Self. Then set your intention for the night. For example, visualise waking up feeling vital, happy, refreshed, revitalized and enthusiastic about your day while being in alignment all day long and seeing yourself going to bed happy and fulfilled.

If you want to accelerate this process and experience many miracles, we recommend you explore the possibilities of joining the Quantum Extra Sensory Perception Masterclass. Joy and Roy Martina developed a new system that allows 'normal' people to connect with the quantum field and, with appropriate training, become full-body channels of information. After the masterclass you will have opened your energy centres and chakras and unlocked your extra sensory perception. Interested? For more info go to: https://bit.ly/quantum-esp.

Wishing you all the blessings you can handle.

Drs Joy and Roy Martina – Miracle Makers

Known worldwide as 'Miracle Makers', Drs Joy and Roy Martina are holistic health experts and leaders in the field of transformational change and the application of quantum science and epigenetics.

About Dr Joy Martina

Dr Joy Martina, psychic psychologist, specialises in teaching intuitive intelligence for entrepreneurs and lay-people. She is a bestselling author, a quantum hypnosis trainer and the creator of many courses including the Christallin Oracle Training, the Joyful Kids Program and the Sleep Your Fat Away Program, to lose weight effortlessly. Her biggest passions are the empowerment of kids and female leadership.

About Dr Roy Martina, MD

Dr Roy Martina MD is a renowned holistic medical doctor, a prolific bestselling author (eighty-eight books), international trainer and keynote speaker and Grandmaster in martial arts. His biggest international best-selling book is Emotional Balance (Hay House). He has worked and taught workshops with Deepak Chopra, Bruce Lipton, Eric Pearl and Masaro Emoto, and he has developed many new holistic therapies and over one thousand natural remedies. His passion is sharing his knowledge and research. As a Quantum Mystic he specialises in the study of the practical application of quantum laws.

Their mission

Together and separately they teach life transforming workshops and retreats worldwide. They are loved for their easy-to-follow techniques, miraculous interventions and refreshing sense of humour. Their mission is to open the hearts and awaken the higher consciousness of millions through the magic of rapid, positive, lasting change also known as miracles!

Joy & Roy Martina Christallin/Quantum Multiverse website: https://www.Christallin.com

Joy Martina website: https://www.JoyMartina.com

Roy Martina website: https://www.RoyMartina.tv

Joy & Roy Martina Quantum Multiverse facebook: https://www.facebook.com/joyandroy/

Joy Martina facebook: https://www.facebook.com/dr.joymartina

Joy Tribe facebook: https://www.facebook.com/groups/thejoytribegroup

Roy Martina facebook: https://www.facebook.com/roy.m.martina

Roy Martina facebook: https://www.facebook.com/roymartinaMD/

Joy & Roy Martina Quantum Multiverse instagram: https://instagram.com/quantummultiversity?igshid=1vd01xfisrylh

Joy Martina instagram: https://instagram.com/drjoymartina

Joy & Roy Martina Quantum Multiverse YouTube: https://youtube.com/c/ChristallinUsjoyandroy

Roy Martina YouTube: https://youtube.com/c/RoyMartinaTV

Joy & Roy Martina Christallin LinkedIn: https://www.linkedin.com/company/christallin

Joy Martina LinkedIn: https://www.linkedin.com/in/%E2%9C%A8%F0%9F%94%AEjoy-martina-%F0%9F%94%AE%E2%9C%A8-175b7454

Roy Martina LinkedIn: https://www.linkedin.com/in/roymartinamd/

SETTING YOURSELF UP FOR EXPANSION

Dr Kim Brown

How Mindset affects Physical health and wellbeing

Have you ever wondered why something in your body didn't really hurt until you noticed the new bruise or the blood coming from it, and then it hurt – A LOT!

Have you ever noticed that your body's aches and pains were significantly increased when you were tired and stressed?

Have you ever noticed that your body's immune system shut down after a significant emotional event and therefore you were quite unwell after a trauma?

I am sure you have had times in your past where your physical body was feeling a hundred years old, and you were not sure why.

Let me show you how important your mindset and internal self-chatter is to your physical performance.

I would love to challenge you right now to pop onto the ground and do ten push-ups. While you do them, talk to yourself in the worst possible way. Tell yourself how hopeless you are, that you are useless, that you are weak, that you are not good enough. Be brutal. Be unfair. Be nasty to yourself.

How did it feel? Was it hard? Did it hurt? Were you able to do the push-ups? Or did you fail at them?

Now I want you to completely scrap those feelings and ideas and do another ten pushups with the best self-talk ever. This is easy. I am strong. I am amazing. I am the creator of my destiny. I am the best. I am courageous. Whatever self-talk feels really good for you.

Feel the difference between the two sets of push-ups? Did you succeed this time? Was it easy?

Whether you are Wonder Woman or not, you will have noticed the difference between the two sets of push-ups. The first set would have been tough, even if push-ups are a normal workout for you. The second set would have been so much easier, even though you had already done the initial set and therefore would have been more fatigued for the second set.

Why?

It's quite simple really! The way you talk to yourself significantly changes your body's ability to perform. If you have just told yourself you are not good enough, your body listens! If you have told yourself you are absolutely good enough and strong enough, your body listens!

Here's a very quick science lesson to explain how this works. Neurotransmitters bathe every cell of the body. So if your eyes see something that is scary, it will send the feeling of fear to every part of the body. That's why your heart rate increases, your breathing becomes shallow and your whole body will tingle or you get 'jelly legs'. It's all connected! It's the same mechanism when you feel the overwhelming sense of love or excitement or intense gratitude. All parts of your body feel it, not just your mind.

Therefore if your mind and your mindset has been affected, your physical body and wellbeing will also be affected. This is also the case for illnesses in your body. If a doctor or person of authority gives you a label, a diagnosis and it comes with a prognosis, there is a good chance your body will respond to the upsetting news. Some diseases in the body are even created this way! You may not have had the condition prior to the diagnosis, however, your body may just manifest it simply by the idea being planted in your mind by an authority.

When you're fearful or anxious, your body lives in the 'fight and flight' sympathetic system which increases adrenaline and has your body living in stress. Long term fear or anxiety will create chronic stress and inflammation as ongoing doses of cortisol, the stress hormone, are released.

When you're angry, your body's stress system is heightened and you become short-tempered or short-fused. Your immune system depresses for hours at a time and your energy levels become like a roller coaster of uppers and downers. You may find it much harder to shake off a simple cold or tummy upset, and your body may develop other symptoms like rashes or headaches which are simply due to the increase in long term anger, rage and frustration.

I could give a million examples. However, it is really clear, when your mindset is not in a peak state through either acute or chronic stressful circumstances, then your physical health is affected. Whatever is happening internally, your body represents externally.

Your physical body is often giving you clues as to what emotional issue is going on for you. Author Louise Hay wrote in her book *You can Heal your Life* that 'we create every so-called illness in our body'. Louise gives a list of examples as to how resentment, criticism and guilt are the most harmful emotions that live in our body and that 'releasing resentment will dissolve even cancer'.

Did you know that lower back pain is a fear of money and a lack of financial support? Imagine changing your money mindset and your relationship with how you perceive money. It will not only directly affect your financial abundance, but it will also release your lower back pain as well! Extraordinary!

If your physical troubles are repeating themselves on the left side of the body, be sure to check your feminine connections. Your relationships with your mother, sister or other significant females in your life. If your physical issues are on the right side of your body, check your masculine connections and energies. What past trauma or event are you still holding negative emotion towards on your masculine side? Understanding this relationship can significantly alter your physical wellbeing by concentrating on healing and releasing any pain or trauma related to those gender relationships. This can be a game changer for so many people!

What can we do about it?

You can now appreciate that your mindset affects your physical health and wellbeing. But what can you do about your mindset and releasing the past in order to create vital physical health?

Many people turn to incantations and affirmations, however this relies on repeating positive self-talk within your own head and only affects the conscious mind. The conscious mind is like our battery pack, our filter, our willpower and our logical mind. It only accounts for 5 per cent of our mind's power. However, if you have ever tried to succeed with a New Year's resolution by willpower alone, you know that you are fighting a losing battle!

The reality is, all change needs to happen within the unconscious mind, not the conscious mind. The unconscious mind is where our memories, beliefs, values, habits and behaviours are stored, so if you want to change your long-term thought patterns and your neurology, you need to change it within the unconscious mind. The unconscious mind is also the control centre for the physical body.

It is responsible for our heart beating 100,000 times a day without us having to think about it. It sorts out our digestion, our breathing and all bodily functions without us having to remember to do it consciously (thank goodness!)

There are several modalities out there that can help change the long-term beliefs and values that are stored within the unconscious mind. The most effective, fast and long-lasting modalities that I have experienced are NLP (neurolinguistic programming), hypnosis and Time Line Therapy®. These extraordinary modalities are fairly pain free because it is not required for the person to relive past traumas in order to release them from the neurology. Imagine being able to release the beliefs of 'I am not good enough' and 'I am not worthy' without having to relive the content details of the event that created that belief system in the first place! Game changing!

It is also one of the safest and most effective ways to release negative emotions of anger, sadness, fear, hurt and guilt from your neurology. This is powerful, as these emotions are directly related to heightened cholesterol, heart attacks, anxiety, PTSD and depressed immune system, just to name a few.

Changing your identity

How often has someone asked, 'How are you?' and your default response was 'I'm tired' or 'Busy'?

Can you appreciate that this is exactly what you're embedding into your unconscious mind?

What if your response was 'I am energised' or 'I am productive'? Can you feel the difference? Even if it wasn't perfectly true at the time, it's a far more empowering response than the usual default, and therefore your body will eventually catch up with your brain's message. Why re-embed tired or busy as a default? Do you really want to be known as the person who is always tired? Or always busy? Are you really busy? Or just not yet productive?

The way you talk to yourself on the inside directly reflects on the outside.

Let's say you were considering yourself as an overweight person, and the inner self-talk was 'I am fat.' If you were to change just a simple phrase within the language to 'I have fat', the way your unconscious mind would hear that is changed from a negative disempowering place to an empowering place of possibility. Having fat that could be released rather than *being* fat as an identity is so much more positive and empowering. This gives your physical body permission to be able to let go of the unwanted body fat rather than holding on to it because it's part of your identity. See the difference?

It will take a little practice to change the way you express yourself to others because the old way has been well practised. However, with a little thought and effort, you can catch yourself when you are using disempowering language about yourself and reframe it to something your unconscious mind would like to hear over and over again. This is how we change our physical health and wellbeing. It starts from within our mind because our body will then make the changes that it's been embedded with. Once the conscious and unconscious mind work together with the same integrated beliefs, the physical body will reflect the inner health.

The health of our mental and emotional bodies are truly reflected by our physical body. Change your thoughts and the identity you hold for yourself, and you can change your state of wellbeing.

Dr Kim Brown

Dr Kim Brown is an osteopath, a globally recognised NLP trainer (neurolinguistic programming), hypnosis trainer and Time Line Therapy® trainer who is obsessed with empowering people to thrive emotionally, physically and financially.

When the global financial crisis destroyed her and her husband's personal training business in 2009, she set on a mission to secure multiple income streams within the health and wellness industry and to teach and empower others to do the same. Kim returned to university to get her master's degree in health science (osteopathy) and bachelor of science degree, in order to secure her employment opportunities within the allied health sector. Over years of treating patients, she has become fascinated with the connection between physical pain, financial pain, emotional baggage and the effects of stress and anxiety.

Kim teaches her students and assists her coaching clients to release negative emotions and limiting beliefs from their neurology so they don't carry the generational baggage into their future. She then empowers them with skills to maintain emotional and financial intelligence and to live a stress, anxiety and pain free life of their choosing.

Awards

Top ten female life coaches in Australia, 2021 (fourth)

Website: www.drkimbrown.com
Instagram: @drkimbrown
Facebook: https://www.facebook.com/kim.brown.180625
LinkedIn: Kim Brown

MAGNETISE AND AMPLIFY YOUR BRAND THROUGH THE ART OF PARTNERSHIPS

Carly Faragher

The quality of your life is determined by the quality of your relationships.

– Carly Faragher

It was a dream come true experiencing Burning Man for the first time in 2018. A nine-day gathering in the Nevada Desert (dubbed the playa), where close to 80,000 people cocreate on 1,500+ theme camps, to experience 1,000+ art installations, workshops, performances, music, rides, dressing up and different modes of transport.

The remarkable thing about the temporary Black Rock City, is experiencing thousands of people coming together to share their gifts with one another, with no money exchange system.

Burning Man's gifting economy is governed by ten principles and is an incredible demonstration of how partnerships can work. It is an inspiration for my life and my business. But it wasn't an easy road to get there. I had to experience burnout, in order to set off in search of transformational experiences like this.

There have been pivotal moments in my life that have led me to understand that good relationships are fundamental for fulfillment.

And that through the art of relationship building, anyone can set their business up for long term success, with profitable partnerships.

So, what is a partnership?

A partnership is an arrangement where parties agree to cooperate to advance their mutual interests. Partnerships can be tailored to suit your business and client. Generally speaking, a contra partnership is where products and services are exchanged in lieu of money. An affiliate partnership is where there is commission or a referral fee. And a paid partnership is normally an agreement to do something in return for branding and marketing privileges.

But here's the best kept secret. Anything you do or want to do to grow your business can become a partnership! Speaking, events, Facebook Groups, exchanging services, anything!

Why would you want to use partnerships in your business?

A big risk for business owners is wearing so many hats. Struggling with time management and feeling stressed and overwhelmed, not knowing what to focus on, where to upskill and what to outsource. By partnering with likeminded people, to pool resources and exchange services, you can achieve your desired outcomes twice as fast, with twice as much fun! And even better if your partners are engaging with your ideal audience too, because this opens up the opportunity for them to endorse you to their network.

It can be a serious struggle for business owners to generate leads. Online marketing and advertising can be overwhelming and does not provide a guaranteed return on the investment. There are high ongoing costs. And in an ever-changing online world, with platforms like Facebook constantly updating their algorithms and rules, a lot is out of our control. Partnerships provide certainty.

No matter what happens with the state of the world, or with unknowns like social media, relationships will always be fundamental to business success. We are more connected online than ever before, yet people are craving deep connection and more organic ways of doing business. Partnerships are your opportunity to do business in a way that is authentic and feels good, with people you want to do business with. Having the right partnerships in place is the best competitive advantage for the longevity of your business, because it sets you up for success by having consistent leads.

What types of partnerships would be beneficial in your business?

Partnerships are win-win working relationships. They can come in so many different shapes and sizes, and the incredible thing is, once you understand the formula, you can tailor them to grow your business exponentially!

I fell into management and partnerships, unexpectedly, back in 2010, after just six weeks into a role as events and marketing assistant, when my manager quit and wasn't replaced. I instantly reported to the CEO, and it was sink or swim. I was working for a not-for-profit, and I was the only one in my department, so I very quickly learnt the best way I was going to get support was to make our events profitable so I could fund my team.

Being a creative, I got resourceful, and being a people person, I created opportunities for people and businesses to get what they wanted (if they paid for it!). By identifying what people wanted and the value it was to them, I was able to easily sell to them. If they wanted to pay for things we weren't doing, I tailored the offer and charged a premium for it. If they didn't have a budget, I made sure it was a win-win contra arrangement that helped save me time, energy and money, and added value to our members.

These arrangements came in the form of affiliates, event sponsorships, event profiling such as speaking opportunities, joint events, and marketing opportunities like newsletter advertising and website listings.

By the end of my seven-year journey with this organisation, I had grown my team to five, expanded the events calendar tenfold, contributed to doubling the membership, and created a very profitable business development arm for the organisation.

How can you identify partnerships in your business?

Getting clear on your ideal avatar client, will determine the types of audiences your ideal avatar partner will be engaging with. By doing this, you can also discover the types of clients that can be affiliate partners. You can also do a resources inventory, a stocktake on your most precious resources – your time, energy and money – to see where you can create opportunities to partner with people in the areas where you are most out of balance.

Can you think of the people in your existing network who share your ideal audience who run events, have a podcast, have a Facebook group, have a product or service that your community would be interested in? Or are there things you're spending too much time, energy or money on in your business, that you could outsource through a contra partnership? These are some of the ways you can identify partnerships in your business.

What is one thing you could do to transform your relationships into partnerships?

Burning Man in Black Rock City is known to many as 'home', simply because of how it makes people feel. People have the freedom to be whoever they want to be, wear whatever they want to wear, and do whatever they want to do.

I remember my first day on the playa, setting off to explore the ginormous adult playground, in my bedazzling outfit, on my jazzed-up bicycle. The first encounter I had with someone (who was dressed as a unicorn, in true Burning Man style), I realised I didn't yet have a player name, so they dubbed me Salty Dingo because they said I looked like an Aussie surfer girl!

I met people from all different walks of life and the remarkable thing was how the conversations went. I didn't know their real name, or where they were from, and I didn't know what they did for a living. But I did know what was bringing them joy at Burning Man because they were always so excited to share, and they were always so willing to help if I needed it.

Burning Man principles, like radical self-expression, gifting and radical inclusion, lifted all veils of ulterior motives and preconceived ideas of who someone was. Relating to people from this place of love, acceptance, curiosity and service was like nothing I had ever experienced before, and it completely shifted my way of connecting with people.

I practise this in my business, and with every conversation I end with one simple question that I guarantee will improve the quality and longevity of any relationship and will open up so many opportunities. I ask people 'Is there anything you're looking for help with that would really make a difference in your business or your life right now?'

You see, people always have at least one problem they're trying to solve, and they value people who can help them solve it. Whether you're the one to help them or not, by taking an interest you show you care. This increases your likeability and shows you are trustworthy, which means they're more likely to do business with you.

You don't need to have a solution then and there, nor do you have to commit to helping them, but you can offer to think about it and see if there's any way you or anyone you know might be able to help.

Asking this question then also opens up the opportunity for them to ask you the same question. This then allows you to share something you think they might be able to help you with. If they can't help they might know someone who could. You just never know who they might know!

So, how can you work with me?

During my decade and a half in this field, I have identified key areas which are critical for profitable partnerships, and I have developed them into these into resources and programs that can support you and help your business to flourish.

I work with people one-on-one and one-to-many, and, through my business Hello There, I provide a platform for collaborations and partnership opportunities through speaking, podcasting and events.

I am offering readers access to the Hello There community for FREE, for a limited time, where you can:

- experience networking like never before and develop relationships in a way that feels good for you
- connect with your tribe of wellness and personal development professionals all over the world
- pitch and share yourself and your business so you can expand your brand
- have access to events and podcasts so you can easily get on more stages
- learn successful tips and processes used by organisations like TEDx on how to grow your business through speaking, events and partnerships
- hear the latest teachings from Mindvalley and Dr De Martini coaches, and more
- master the art of transforming relationships into profitable partnerships through various partnership programs
- attend exclusive events including global virtual pitching and matchmaking events.

I would love to have you join the Hello There community. Sign up to gain FREE access here: http://eepurl.com/gpDWjn. I look forward to connecting with you soon!

> The success of your business is determined by the quality of your partnerships.
> – Carly Faragher

Carly Faragher

Carly Faragher is a highly sought-after partnerships strategist, brand expander, business matchmaker, event curator and talent agent. She is also an award-winning fashion designer and founder and director of Hello There, a community for connection, collaboration and expansion.

For over a decade Carly has enjoyed curating, directing and collaborating on hundreds of events all around the world, with thousands in attendance, including for the National Retail Association as their director of events, marketing and partnerships for seven years.

There was a turning point for Carly at the age of thirty, where a build-up of work and family stress resulted in burnout and the need to take a break from the corporate world. She travelled for a year and a half, growing and healing through experiences like a ten-day silent retreat and Burning Man. And it was this inner journey and these unique experiences that are inspiration for Carly's life and business today.

Having held positions with close to forty committees and charities over the past decade and a half, she is a true community leader. She loves to connect people, personalities and businesses together, in order to maximise personal, business and financial potential.

Carly understands the meaning of your network being your net worth, and has facilitated business growth opportunities and partnerships for organisations like TEDxMelbourne as their head of partnerships.

Carly knows what getting your inspired mission in front of a big audience can do for your brand and financial growth, having worked with clients like Mindvalley, World Vision, Hallmark and Salesforce.

Carly is passionate about sharing events, speaking and partnership opportunities with the Hello There Community. She hosts regular global pitching and matchmaking events that unite leaders and business owners in wellness and self-mastery.

Carly is busy currently teaching clients how to have maximum impact and organically grow their business, through the art of profitable partnerships.

List of qualifications:

- Events and project management
- Neuroscience of leadership
- Fashion design and marketing
- Student of Mindvalley, Tony Robbins, William Whitecloud and Landmark

Work with Carly:

Join the Hello There community for your free brand expanding opportunities here: http://eepurl.com/gpDWjn

Website: www.hello-there.com.au
Instagram: https://www.instagram.com/carlyfaragher/
Facebook: https://www.facebook.com/carly.faragher.98/
LinkedIn: https://www.linkedin.com/in/carly-faragher/

DECODE AND UPLEVEL

INTRODUCTION

Tracey Jewel

When you step up your game, your life will level up!

You may have heard the term 'uplevel' floating around on the Internet, and I think it's an excellent way to describe moving up to a place higher than where you once were. Growth and 'upleveling' has always been a top value of mine. This isn't always upping my skills or income, it could be, for example, being more grateful than I was the week before, being more present today than yesterday or being able to overcome a challenge more easily than before.In this final section, we're going to cleanse and upgrade every aspect of your life – your relationships, home, finances, even your environmental footprint. We'll release fears, worries and the stresses weighing you down. As more and more high-vibrational energy begins to course through your system, you'll start to embody the radiant and powerful being you indeed are – even if that version of you seems out of reach right now.

What does it mean to uplevel your life?

To uplevel your life means a few things:

- being better than you were in the past
- letting go of what holds you back
- letting go of self-sabotaging behaviour
- not living life on autopilot
- making choices and decisions that align with the bigger vision you have for your life.

Maybe this still sounds a little 'woo-woo' to you. But I believe you also have a voice in your head telling you that you could be doing something greater with your life. A simple analogy that relates to upleveling or *leveling up* is playing a video game. You improve your skills with each level you play, learning as you go how to move to the next level once you've conquered the particular stage you're at.

There are countless ways to live an upleveled life that focuses on bringing intention and positive change into your life. Before we explore upleveling in more detail, here are some areas and ideas to consider:

1. Mindset

- Improve the way you speak to and think about yourself.
- Expand upon what you believe is possible for yourself.
- Focus on the current moment rather than the past or future.

2. Values

- Identify your top five values and what they mean to you.
- Commit to activities, experiences, and people who uphold your values.
- Keep your values written in a visible place so you are reminded of them often.

3. Vision

- Write down your vision for the future and what you would like to achieve.
- Set goals for yourself that align with that vision.
- Revisit your vision often so you are reminded of your intentions.

4. Habits

- Commit to daily habits that align with your values and vision.
- Develop a morning routine that nourishes mind, body and soul.
- Set daily intentions that encourage you to keep showing up in your life.

5. Plans

- Plan action steps that align with your goals.
- Map out your daily and weekly workflows.
- Focus on sticking to the plans you set for yourself.

6. Actions and Decision Making

- Make action-based choices that align with your values and priorities.
- Listen to your inner guidance when making decisions.
- Get out of your own head and take imperfect action.

7. Discipline

- Hold yourself accountable to your intentions.
- Stop wasting time with distractions and procrastination.
- Set clear boundaries with your time and energy.

Action Step:

Review the list above and make a note of the things you want to work on. Regularly revisit your notes as a reminder to be more intentional with what you choose to do on a daily basis.Now let's dive deeper and uplevel even more …

SURVIVING ... TO HIGH VIBIN

Carol King

There is nothing more important to true growth than realising that you are not the voice of the mind – you are the one who hears it.
– Michael Singer

The life I'm living now is the life that I always dreamed of. But when I was younger, fear controlled my life, my relationships and my thinking. Throughout my childhood and teenage years, my subconscious ran self-destructive, automatic programs: negative belief systems that stripped me of my confidence, happiness and wellbeing.

As an adult, I needed to learn how to heal my inner world so I didn't continually push away the people the universe sent to help me and love me. My low vibrational energy was palpable – and not in a good way. My anger, frustration and anxiety could be sensed by everyone around me. To change my life, I had to understand the mind-body connection and its shared language of communication. I needed to change my low-level energy and my destructive, subconscious patterns.

By changing my thinking and feeling, over time I could change my behaviour.

I studied to become a clinical hypnotherapist, using clinical hypnotherapy, a method of using the 'natural' hypnotic state as a powerful therapeutic tool to overcome life's obstacles. As a powerful therapeutic intervention, hypnotherapy can frequently bring about rapid and beneficial change in a very spontaneous manner, by accessing the subconscious mind. In the hypnotic state, the subconscious mind is receptive to positive suggestion and can bring about lasting change at a deeper level.

Through the study of addictions, I realised I was using addictive patterns to distract myself from the fear, pain and emptiness I felt inside. Subconsciously, I was escaping my pain and discomfort and disconnecting from myself and others. At the same time, my addictive patterns and behaviours gave me the sense of comfort, familiarity, peace and control I so desperately craved.

To make my life work, I had to stop listening to the negative, persistent, self-destructive voice in my head. My demanding, unrealistic expectations were the cause of my unhappiness, anxiety, resentment and anger – which were automatically triggered when I, as well as other people and situations, did not fit my impossible expectations. It was the patterns in my mind that were making me unhappy, although I projected them onto others, blaming them instead.

I created a practice that allowed me to manage my emotional demands and destructive, inner programming. When I felt triggered, I would close my eyes, take a few deep, calming breaths and ask myself:

- Do I want my happiness to be dependent on other people and the outside world?

- Is it really other people and the outside world that are creating my unhappiness?
- Can I 'prefer' for something to happen in a certain way and, if it doesn't happen, still be happy?
- Do I want to be right, or do I want to be happy?

When I began choosing happiness, my mind would slow, become calmer, and I would feel a sense of peace inside my body and an inner spaciousness open up. From a state of presence, I could allow my mind to create 'preferences' instead of demands, and eventually become detached from demanding specific expectations and outcomes.

To continue changing my inner and outer worlds, I needed to focus on raising my level of consciousness. By bringing attention and awareness to my automatic programming, I began to disconnect from lower-level vibrational frequencies of consciousness – guilt, fear and anger. I began to experience myself and life through the emotional lens of allowing higher vibrational frequencies of happiness, love, joy and bliss.

At first, my experiences of these higher levels of consciousness felt uncomfortable and unfamiliar. I had lost hope in my dreams, and the disappointment of life often felt overwhelming. I was terrified of letting go, trusting life and allowing happiness into my life.

For years, I had struggled with shame, fear, anger, hopelessness, chronic anxiety, digestive disorders and muscle tension. Unknowingly, I had dysregulated my nervous system's adaptive response to fight-flight-freeze, and its prolonged, long-term, switched on outcomes. I had subconsciously been manifesting unpleasant hyperarousal and hypervigilant symptoms. Often the fight and flight or freeze response would continue for days, weeks and months, long after my perceived threat had gone. When the freeze response persisted, I would shut down to self-protect, becoming more susceptible to dissociation, anxiety and depression.

By practising the following meditation techniques, I learnt a way to rebalance my nervous system and manage my dissociation, anxiety and depression. These meditations helped change my energy from a freeze state into a more fluid state, where I could release anger, fear, shock and trauma, all the heavy dense states and energy frequencies.

- Focused Meditation: Concentrate or focus on a sound, an image or a mantra. The key is to engage your senses.
- Mindfulness Meditation: Becoming aware of thoughts, feelings, and sensations as they arise. Don't judge them; just observe. You may also combine noticing your breath whilst observing thoughts, feelings or body sensations.
- Movement Meditation: Walking, deep breathing, swimming, dancing, shaking or laughing. This type of meditation is important to free us from the contraction, the shutdown and the freezing that trauma can cause, and helps free our minds and bodies.

Using self-hypnosis and meditation techniques, I began tuning into higher energies and frequencies of abundance, peace, joy and love. Maintaining a still, peaceful inner world, allowed me to connect and become comfortable with my own personal vibrational frequency. By creating new daily intentions, I was beginning to let go of my old, stuck, self-limiting beliefs and programming. I was teaching my brain to make new neurological patterns and new, feelgood chemicals for my body. I was finally changing my brain chemistry and my biology, just by thinking differently. I was learning that information, energy, and consciousness are all connected. I was creating new states of being and healing my body. By changing my energy field, I was changing my personality and eventually my personal reality.

DAILY EXERCISE

Observing the Wandering Mind: Becoming aware of your thoughts
(Write down your answers in a journal)

Throughout the day, regularly ask yourself:

- What am I thinking right now?
- Are these thoughts true?
- What do I believe/not believe about these thoughts?
- How often do I experience these thoughts?
- What emotions am I aware of when I experience these thoughts?
- Are these thoughts relevant right now?

I allowed myself to fail and have bad days. I experienced inner battles around letting go of my old, negative, stubborn beliefs and accepting new ones that would contradict the old. On some days, my negative, critical inner voice would return, creating havoc and confusion. I would constantly remind myself that the voice was just negative beliefs playing in my head like a stuck record player. It was not 'who I am'. On those days, I was gentle and kind with myself, allowing plenty of rest, sleep, meditation and gentle exercise.

By allowing myself to just observe and be present, I would watch my thoughts, my feelings and my reactions without getting lost in them. Learning to embrace the present moment, through meditation and self-hypnosis took me out of my troubled, racing mind and into a portal of quiet, empty spaciousness. By embracing the present moment, I found all my unhappiness and struggle simply dissolved. By simply watching without judgement whatever I was experiencing on the inside, its energy would disappear after only a few minutes. By accepting fully where I was at, without trying to change anything, I would automatically be taken into a state of peace.

I still practise the following exercise several times each day to bring me into a place of presence and acceptance.

DAILY EXERCISE

Bringing Acceptance to Every Emotion

- Sit quietly and comfortably and tune into your body.
- Become aware of what you are feeling right now.
- Allow yourself to simply observe whatever you feel inside your body.
- Just observe and fully accept whatever you feel inside your body.
- Observe without any judgment. Notice what you observe.
- Don't try to change anything.
- Very often after a few minutes these emotions simply dissolve or disappear.

The battle got easier each day, until I sensed the universe gently urging me to leave my relationship.

Once again, I sensed inner resistance and refusal to trust and let go. Six months later, my life began to unravel at an alarming speed. I had to give up my home as the owners needed to move in. I was devasted. My home was my fortress and had kept me safe through these past years. I wasn't ready to let go. I knew my life situation was being stripped away, but, gripped by fear, I continued to cling. I continued to sense the gentle guidance of the universe and knew I was being called to surrender and let go completely at a deeper level than ever before. Trusting the universe, I took a leap of faith.

I quit my job and, a few weeks later, moved back to Western Australia.

Back home in Western Australia, I allowed myself to connect deeper with my feelings and let them 'just be', without judgment or trying to change them in any way. I began experiencing a state of deep calmness and inner peace that I had never felt before. I knew I was connecting and experiencing life at deeper levels and higher vibrations.

Being on my own was often terrifying. My addictive thoughts and behavioural patterns surfaced once again, and emotional trauma memories from my past became triggered, bringing fear, anger, numbness, hopelessness and anxiety into my life.

Needing a way to self-soothe and calm my turbulent thoughts and emotions, whilst keeping my unreasonable demands in check, I created the following exercise and used it every time I began to lose control. It helped me to quieten my mind and bring my awareness back to the present moment, often diffusing a potentially destructive situation.

DAILY EXERCISE

Being Aware: Managing addictive thoughts and demands

(Write down your answers in a journal)

Use this technique whenever possible, to avoid overreacting to a trigger in your environment or losing your awareness and slipping into your negative, destructive subconscious patterns.

- Sit quietly and comfortably. Take a few slow, deep breaths and allow yourself to relax.
- Become aware of your thoughts right now.
- Are these thoughts critical, judgmental and demanding of yourself or others in any way?

- Did you feel you have a choice to change your thinking or choose different thoughts?
- Did you intend to act differently, but your familiar automatic patterns/addictive behaviours were too powerful to overcome?
- How long have these thought patterns/addictive behaviours been occurring?
- Does anyone in your family have similar patterns/addictive behaviours?
- What does the energy feel like in your body right now?
- What emotions are you aware of right now?

One day, in the middle of meditating, I felt the Universe encouraging me to leap, to jump off a 'metaphorical' cliff, to just fly and float and it would catch me, support me. I could feel the fear rise up within me, but a greater part of me truly wanted to try it, to let go and trust completely, but didn't know how. Not knowing 'how' had always been a stumbling block. Often, because I lived and reacted out of fear, I would never allow myself to try something new.

Suddenly, I realised that it wasn't about knowing what or how to 'do' something, it was just about allowing, about letting go of control and simply trusting. There was no 'doing' at all. I knew that if I didn't take the step, the universe would show me an alternate path – not necessarily the smooth, peaceful path it was offering. So, I just took a step of faith and said, 'I let go!' and imagined myself flying and floating. And the universe supported me completely. I had never felt so free in my entire life.

Unless we can learn to quieten and tame the mind, we cannot move beyond the limited self and discover our true, higher being. We have an internal GPS guiding us, expanding us to be all we are capable of being, expanding our awareness. Our experience of life and self is a manifestation of what we think life is. We either trust life or we don't.

We are the designers of our inner worlds. We create our own internal states. Our identity shapes our reality. Enjoy being in the moment. Listen to the moment. Sense the spaciousness. Observe the spaciousness. Don't be in a rush to fill it up.

In my hypnotherapy practice, Healy and hypnotherapy are my therapeutic power tools. Together, alongside meditation, they support clients in managing trauma, subconscious patterns, belief systems and trauma memories that are keeping them stuck.

Hypnotherapy, meditation and Healy frequency programs provide an integrated approach for clients to balance their bioenergetic field, support their mental and emotional balance, and promote bioenergetic balance, vitality and overall wellbeing.

To connect with me and find out more about my story, products and services go to: www.justvibe.com.au.

Carol King

Carol King is an experienced certified clinical hypnotherapist, counsellor and trainer, with passion and vision for helping others overcome childhood and personal issues, and self-destructive patterns and blockages that often prevent the achievement of happy, loving relationships, successful careers and personal freedom and transformation.

Born in Glasgow, Scotland, Carol began her career in business and hospitality. A move to Australia in 1992 prompted a change to corporate training and sales management.

Inspired to overcome her personal, medical and relationship issues, Carol began transforming her life through studying counselling, clinical hypnotherapy and meditation, the keys to her freedom, success and self-awareness.

At age forty, Carol experienced an aha moment that changed her life forever, the realisation that 'you are not the voice of the mind, you are the one who hears it'.

Having struggled for decades, trying to change and control people and situations, Carol learnt how to change herself. She teaches others that lasting freedom, transformation and happiness come by answering one important question: 'Do I want to be right, or do I want to be happy?'

Clients benefit from her gentle, unique approach, assisting them on their pathway to freedom and joy.

Carol integrated Healy into her hypnotherapy practice to complement and enhance a safe, nurturing pathway and healing environment.

Hypnotherapy and Healy are Carol's 'power tools' of therapy, which accelerate the body's and mind's capacity to change and self-heal.

Carol's qualifications include: Advanced Diploma Clinical Hypnotherapy, Certificate IV Counselling, Certificate IV Training and Assessment and Diploma in Business Management.

Special offer:

Hypnotherapy and Healy Offer – All-in-One Energy Healing Therapy

Enjoy 50% discount: 90-minute session (valued at $250) that includes FREE Healy scans, 60 minutes hypnotherapy (face to face or online) and FREE Energy Healing Meditation

OR

Hypnotherapy and Emotional Trauma Therapy Offer

Enjoy 50% discount: 3 hour session (valued at $475) that includes 90 minutes hypnotherapy (face to face or online) and 90 minutes Emotional Trauma Therapy session, including FREE Emotional Trauma Assessment.

Websites: www.justvibe.com.au & www.naturaltherapypages.com.au/connect/carol-king-therapies/about_me/42058
Instagram: www.instagram.com/carol.king.3745/
Facebook: www.facebook.com/CarolKingTherapies
LinkedIn: www.linkedin.com/public-profile/in/carol-king-9a42a35b/

ALIGNING WITH YOUR TRUE PURPOSE

Vanessa Indovino

Can you remember who you were, before the world told you who you should be?

– Charles Bukowski

In 2014, whilst riding my scooter around the winding roads of Ulluwatu, Bali, I came across a stray dog in a dead-end street. Having heard all sorts of stories about Bali dogs, and with the dog walking towards me barking, I quickly turned the bike around and sped off. Sensing my fear, the dog pursued me aggressively. As the distance between the dog and my bike lessened, my fear increased. I picked up speed, realising that if I crashed, the dog may attack me. A micro-second thought may have saved me from an attack.

In that short second it occurred to me that whatever was meant to happen would happen. This was all that was needed for me to surrender and keep the bike steady. Eventually, the dog gave up its chase. Whether that dog was dangerous or not I will never know, yet I look back now and realise the encounter was symbolic of the fear that had driven me for a large portion my adult life. By surrendering to the dog and, metaphorically, the uncertainty of life, I came to realise I cannot control what I do not know.

Fear became pivotal in my corporate career, manifesting itself in the form of anxiety, stress and, eventually, burnout. I have been a high achiever my whole life, always striving to be better and do better. High achievers put an enormous amount of pressure on themselves, and I was no different. I over-extended myself in ways that weren't necessary and were detrimental to my mental health, pushing myself to the point where I was stressed and anxious. School and work had always been a priority because I learnt to associate achieving with receiving approval, love, recognition and praise. I had to succeed and do well because, on a very deep subconscious level, if I didn't, it meant that I was not loveable, not worthy and therefore I was not enough. This was the story I played out. For me, the drive to succeed was almost a survival mechanism. My self-worth hung on my grades and my work. Through my achievements, I felt enough. Later in life, I realised this is far from the truth.

The perception of success

This paradigm of success is nothing new. All of us are born into a world that conditions us to be passive and obedient. By doing what our parents, teachers and society tells us, we receive recognition and praise and we're labelled as 'good' boys or girls. These labels condition us to constantly seek validation, continuing into the workforce and our relationships as we grow older. We're not empowered and encouraged to follow our heart and do what we truly desire. Instead, we're told to find a job that pays well and offers long-term security. We're programmed to follow the crowds, to do socially acceptable things like go to university, chase after money and status. This striving mentality leads us to continually push, even when our body is resisting, and say yes to opportunities that aren't aligned. This was my path and the path of many other women I know, and so it's no wonder so many feel trapped in their professional careers. The path they're walking is not one of their choosing, they've simply been programmed this way. With this awareness and clarity, it is possible to create a new path for yourself, one of your own design.

After graduating from university with a double degree in marketing and psychology, I took my first corporate job in marketing. Despite the whispering inner voice that was telling me this didn't feel aligned, I persevered for over a decade, working for various national and multinational organisations. I climbed the corporate ladder with a lot of success. I built great relationships and learnt invaluable skills. On the outside, I had it all. But something was missing. I had been searching outside of myself for this illusive sense of happiness and fulfillment that I was conditioned to believe would come at the next promotion or when I landed the next big job. Yet I was faced with the exact opposite. I felt empty and disillusioned. I suffered quietly, desperately craving deeper meaning in my work and life but not knowing where or who to turn to. On the weekends, I would use alcohol and partying to escape how I was feeling. It was a vicious cycle. The insurmountable pressures and demands of work, combined with this feeling of unfulfillment, led me to experience my own challenging journey of anxiety and burnout. I remember the feeling distinctly: tightness in my chest, exhaustion, physical symptoms such as mouth ulcers and difficulty sleeping. I had lost all purpose and excitement for life. That inner voice became so loud, I couldn't ignore it. I had two choices: continue to suffer down this path or venture into the unknown and create a new possibility for myself. At the time I had been offered a promotion, but no carrot would have been enticing enough for me to stay, so I declined the offer and resigned from my corporate job that same day.

Surrendering into the unknown

In January 2014, I made a decision that completely changed the course of my life. I sold all my belongings and booked a one-way ticket to Bali. The mysterious Island of the Gods was calling me back. Any uncertainty or fear that I had was overridden with an intense sense of curiosity and excitement. I had no set plans; all I had was my passport and unwavering faith and belief that there was a better life out there for me. My thirst for self-improvement took me on journey of self-discovery where I practiced with mentors in yoga, meditation, embodiment and energy healing. I stopped drinking alcohol and eventually stopped eating meat.

Being surrounded by an abundance of nature and lush tropical energy, I felt completely free and as though I'd come home. I felt healthier, lighter and more connected to myself. I met incredible souls who were living an inspired life guided by their spirit and heart, many working for themselves as coaches, healers, designers and investors. They had the lifestyle I desired, and it gave me a glimpse of what was possible. The Balinese taught me that being content and fulfilled can be achieved with so little, and also to show gratitude through prayer and ritual every day. After spending a year in Bali and travelling throughout South East Asia, I decided to return to Australia where I continued my studies. I pursued different modalities in holistic health and participated in workshops and retreats that transformed me on a very deep level. I went on to become a certified life coach, meditation teacher and reiki practitioner. By committing to myself fully and doing 'the work', I began the process of truly healing from the inside out.

On reflection, I wouldn't change any part of my life. I am grateful for the gifts and lessons each experience has given me. Through pain, I found purpose: to help others, especially women, to transcend their current situation, overcome stress, anxiety and burnout and connect more deeply with themselves and their purpose.

How can you connect to your authentic self and ultimately your purpose?

Living in alignment with your authentic self and your purpose means that you're vibrating at a frequency that matches that of your soul essence, not that of your ego or societal influences. Purpose gives us a true sense of fulfilment that can't be obtained from any material object, leisure activity or achievement. Before you can discover or fully step into your purpose, it's important to go inwards, connect with yourself and release anything that might be getting in the way of you showing up in all of your brilliance. As you begin to understand yourself and your emotions on a deeper level, you'll develop greater clarity on why you're here and how you want to show up. Here are some ways that you can connect with your authentic self today.

Feel your emotions

As young children, we're taught to suppress or hide our emotions. This can leave us feeling numb and disconnected from our bodies. Yet emotions are highly intelligent ways in which the body expresses itself, signalling that something needs attention. It's a call for you to pause and lean in. As Robert Frost said, 'The best way out is always through.' So next time you feel an uncomfortable emotion, rather than distracting yourself with television, work, alcohol or any other diversion, sit and befriend your emotions.

- Label your emotions; simply name what is present. (For example, anger is present, sadness is present.)

- Place a hand on your heart and a hand on your abdomen, and breathe into the emotion. Breathe in for five, hold for seven, breathe out for five. Do this as many times as you need.
- If you feel an emotion surfacing, rather than judge yourself, allow the emotion to express itself through you. You can cry or even scream into a pillow. Create a ritual out of it by lighting a candle and playing some emotive music. This can be a cathartic experience, allowing you to release anything that needs to be shifted.
- Journal out your emotions by freely responding to the following questions: How am I feeling? What am I feeling? This can help you to gain some perspective over your emotions and understand them more clearly.

As soon as you start to bring awareness and love to your emotions and allow them to express themselves, you'll find they have less power over you, and you'll be met with a sense of freedom and relief.

Connect with your body

In high-stress work environments, we can become extremely disconnected from our bodies, and more prone to stress and anxiety. Of all communication, 55 per cent is conveyed through the body, and so verbal communication alone, which makes up only 7 per cent, is limited in expressing emotions. Embodiment and movement practices, such as dance, allow the body to express what is too deep for words, and to release the tension we hold in our body. It's a practice I go to regularly. It's where I can surrender, let go of control and tap into greater levels of clarity and inspiration. We can't always think our way through problems, but by connecting with your body regularly, you allow it to naturally heal itself.

Now it's your turn. I invite you to connect with your essence and the inner child within you that wants to express and dance. Turn on your favourite music or create a playlist that moves you, and allow yourself to let go of the conditioning that's holding you back. If it feels awkward in the beginning, lean into the discomfort and move through the feelings that arise. Dance is one of the fastest ways to change your physiological state. Free yourself and give it a go!

Transform limiting beliefs

The only things holding you back from your own greatness are your limiting beliefs and negative self-talk. The experiences and traumas of our childhood form who we believe we are and what we believe we can and can't do. These beliefs are just stories we tell ourselves. They are not reality. My main belief has been that 'I'm not enough'. It has kept me playing small and safe in many areas of my life. To transform limiting beliefs and begin living to your full potential, you can:

Become aware of how you're speaking to yourself. Awareness creates space between you and the thought. You are no longer the thought. You are the observer.

Journal out your answers to the following powerful questions developed by Byron Katie: Is it true? Can you absolutely know it's true? How do you react – what happens – when you believe that thought? Who would you be without the thought?

Delve deep and look at when that belief first formed. If it was in childhood, start to bring loving kindness to your inner child. You can do this by forming a dialogue with her; look in the mirror and tell her you love her, ask her what she needs or even write a letter to your inner child.

Create new empowering beliefs. Write them down and make it a daily ritual to commit to a new story and a new you!

Get clear on your values

It seems so simple, yet few people choose their values, let alone live in alignment with them. Your values are what you deem important and are intrinsically linked to you living a purposeful life. They influence the decisions you make and determine the direction that your life takes. Lack of awareness around your values can leave you with a false sense of purpose – one that is based on others' expectations. To get clear on your values:

- Identify the times when you were most proud.
- Identify the times when you were most happy. What were you doing? How did you feel?
- Identify the times when you were the most fulfilled and satisfied.
- Based on your above experiences, list fifteen to twenty values – love, freedom, health, discipline, wealth, and so on. Free write without thinking too much about it.
- If there are similar values, group them together and then pick one value in each group that encapsulates the value you live by or want to live by. You should end up with six to eight top values.
- Prioritise those values from highest to lowest. This is critical, because when making a decision, you'll need to evaluate how that scenario aligns with your most important values.

Be honest with yourself. Check in to see whether your current career and life lines up with your values, and make adjustments accordingly.

If you're living in alignment with your values, you're living in your highest expression and truth.

Become curious

Lack of meaning and purpose can also be a trigger that leads to burn-out. So many people settle for unhappy lives, yet they are capable of achieving more meaning simply by adopting an attitude of curiosity. For the most part, I've lived my life with curiosity and an open mind, dedicated to the endless pursuit and search for what lit up my soul. I experimented with many jobs, hobbies and businesses before I found my true passion. I didn't always succeed; I failed forward, grew from the experience and most importantly, I never gave up. I invite you to do the same. Become curious, embrace the unfamiliar, explore, read, research, journal ideas, get creative and always ask questions. What brings you the most joy? What are you naturally good at and what skills come easy to you? Through this process of enquiry, you'll stumble upon passions that you can turn into a profitable career. Always stay open to your desires and interests, and never stop learning and trying new things. Each experience, job and lesson will guide you to where you're meant to be and open you up to more adventure and joy. Hint: Your greatest life challenge can often lead you to your greatest gift and purpose.

Each tool or process I've shared, brings you back to one simple truth: you have everything you need within you. There is nothing outside of you that can make you whole and complete – no job, relationship or material object. You are whole, powerful and worthy right now. Truly believing this will set you free.

Make a choice to choose you!

Your purpose starts with you. Make a choice to step outside your comfort zone and lean into the life you desire. Acknowledge that it can be scary and that it may bring up doubt or other fears, but don't allow the circumstances of your current situation to swallow you up. There is a way out.

Getting real with yourself is the first step to change. Without awareness, you'll continue down the same path. Ask yourself the hard questions: Do you want to continue living your life this way? What is it costing you? Your health? Your family and friends? Make a commitment to yourself to create change now.

You don't need to sacrifice your career or go on a long retreat to find support. I've done the groundwork for you, through practical applications in my own life and that of my clients. I offer a space for you to re-connect with yourself and listen to your own inner wisdom, to let go of what's not serving you, and redesign your life so that you feel inspired and lit up.

If this is resonating with you, feel free to reach out.

You are so worthy of living the life you truly deserve!

Vanessa Indovino

Vanessa is a life coach who supports ambitious women to overcome burnout, anxiety and self-doubt.

Intuitive and compassionate, Vanessa's purpose is to empower women to embrace change so they can live a life where they feel inspired, where they feel free to be themselves and know they are inherently enough. She's the founder of 'Burnout to Breakthrough', a coaching program that supports women to reconnect with themselves and listen to their inner wisdom, to let go of what's not serving them, transform limiting beliefs and manifest their highest vision. Vanessa provides a space for busy women to implement practical and intuitive tools that bring about profound transformations in every area of their life.

With a background in marketing and psychology, Vanessa climbed the corporate ladder for over a decade, working for a range of national and multinational companies. The anxiety and burnout she experienced during this time acted as a catalyst for her to quit her job, embrace uncertainty and embark on a journey of self-discovery. Her desire for a more meaningful life, led her to spend twelve months in Asia practicing with mentors in yoga, mindfulness and energy healing. She then continued her studies in Australia, where she became a certified life coach, mindfulness teacher and reiki practitioner.

Work with Vanessa and receive 10% off her signature coaching program, plus a free 20-minute discovery session.

Website: www.vanessaindovino.com
Instagram: @vanessaindovino
Facebook: www.facebook.com/vanessaindovino

ATTRACTION MARKETING AND MAGNETIZING YOUR DREAM TEAM

Nicole Crowley

You have more magic within you than you could ever imagine and the world is waiting for it, so go out and share it with the courage of a lion!

I have suffered with chronic migraines my entire life. When I went six months migraine-free, I shared the celebration and my excitement with the world through social media. I brought them on my journey with me! I held celebrations all day and hinted at what I would reveal later throughout my posts. I built up the excitement around how my life changed through the Healy, and I sprinkled in scientific facts about it too. I could have started the day with one post about being migraine-free, instead I listened to my intuition and included my audience in the all-day celebration! Attraction marketing and drawing in your dream team starts with trusting your intuition.

Attraction marketing is sharing your offer by providing valuable information about it before convincing customers to buy. I view it more as sharing marketing rather than attraction marketing.

What do you love about your offer? How has it added something to your life? Make a list of all of these things and use this as a map of what to focus on when you post.

Has your offer brought better health, confidence, financial freedom? Share it! What do you love about it? Share the excitement, results and, above all, share your life! Bring your audience into the moment and make it so they can see themselves there too! In doing so, your audience will start connecting the dots, realising how your offer can change their lives, and they will choose to become your customer.

There are a lot of different ways you can share these moments. Use your content as a way to bring your audience into your day! If you achieve stress relief from your offer, share a post about being able to relax with your children instead of running ragged as you used to.

Think of attraction marketing as spoon feeding little bits and pieces of the benefits of what you have to offer, rather than shoving the whole piece of pie in their mouth. This is exactly what it is, it is sharing the benefits throughout your day, and helping them see how it can fit into their lives and benefit them.

The easiest way for someone to see your excitement about what you have to offer is by going live. This is your opportunity to show people why you're excited about what you have to offer. I go live all the time about different ways the Healy has changed my life! When you receive an intuitive pull to share a message or go live, do it and be authentic when you do! If you show up a certain way because you feel this is what they expect of you, but it doesn't feel true to who you are, that energy of discomfort will be reflected in your life. You are receiving that pull for a reason, and there is probably someone who is supposed to connect with you in that exact moment through your content.

Genuine spontaneous excitement when you go live, has further reach than a scripted message every time. One thing to remember is that we are all human. Regardless of our accomplishments, we all have good and bad days. When we realise this, it gives us freedom. It is so freeing when you realise that no one is perfect, and that you are perfect in your imperfection. This gives you the freedom to present the true you, and this will mean so much more to your audience and the people you are trying to attract. This is true about lives as well as posts and stories.

In general, put yourself in the shoes of your audience, and think about what kind of things they would like to see and post those. Post it for the thousands in the future who will be reading it. Post it with the intention that this will reach who it is meant for.

Every single time you post content or go live, focus on the energy you attach to it. Are you posting hoping this might reach someone and bring you a customer? This is setting the intention of lack. Are you posting knowing that every time you post the right people see it, come to you and love what you have to offer? This is operating from a state of belief! This is the intention and the energy you want to match each time you share!

Showing your true authentic self each time you post is one of the most important things about attraction marketing, as well as magnetising your dream team.

Anytime you post you aren't just sharing to share, you are putting your energy out there that will in turn magnetise your dream team to you.

What energy do you want to attract? What is it in you that connects with that energy? Share that! Think about what would make you excited about working with someone? Is it their knowledge about a product, or is it their excitement and fun for life!

How do you magnetise your dream team? The most important thing is determining who your dream team is. What attributes and passions do you want them to have? You want to get very specific on the traits you want in your dream team, as these things will be the foundation of what you share.

Just as important as presenting what you love about your offer, is presenting content they will love. In order to attract a person who is heart-centred, you need to be putting out content that would resonate with them. The most important thing is, if you are wanting to attract heart-centred leaders, ask yourself how you can become a heart-centred leader. How can you present the ways you already are a leader in your life? You don't need to pretend to be a top leader in order to attract them, you just need to display leadership in what you already do. This is also an opportunity for you to assess your energy and say to yourself: What is holding me back from being a leader in order to attract them?

What is usually holding us back from being fully present is our limiting beliefs. There are so many ways to work on your limiting beliefs, but the most important part of this is recognising what they are in the first place. Start thinking about what you admire in others, and next time you think 'man I wish I was like that', guess what – you are! You would not be able to recognise something in someone unless it was already in you. Now look at what is in you and why you haven't recognised it already, that is where the limiting belief lies.

Once you recognise your limiting beliefs, start working through them. You can do this through journaling, meditating, working with quantum frequencies, or clearing the conditioning and patterning that is in you. I always say, when you step into and embrace your fear you are opening a door to your next level.

Attraction marketing and becoming the energy you want to attract takes a lot of self-discovery, which is the exciting part of the journey. As you start discovering more about what has been holding you back from shouting about what you offer from the hilltops, more obstacles start to clear from your path.

Post daily and keep on posting because you never know who is actually paying attention. Post as if you already have your dream team, post as your future self. When you post as your future highest self, everything you're posting will be for the masses of customers and team members you have in the future.

Trust yourself, listen to your intuition and then act on it. If you feel a pull to post something about charity, then do it. When you listen to your intuition and can recognise what your intuition sounds like, this is when the game changes. Your intuition is soft and subtle and there to guide you to your highest self.

Every time you share on social media, you are branding yourself. It is important to remember that any time you comment on someone else's post or reach out to someone, you are still representing your brand.

Join groups where your dream team would hang out, and engage them to build genuine connections. Emotions and intentions can be felt even in a typed message; make sure it is genuine. It is important to connect with the genuine intention of connecting and finding out how you can help one another, not just to sell something. I go into conversations with the intention that I'm so grateful that whatever needs to unfold for each of our highest goods will happen.

As you're putting all of this effort into posting with intention and making sure you are representing your brand, take the extra steps to ensure these efforts are being seen. Do what you need to do to be seen, to work with the algorithms in place. One way to do this is to make sure you post every single day. This doesn't mean posting about your offer every day. Mix in posts about your family, nature or quotes. But make sure to post at least one content piece per day. This is also where you can utilise your stories. One great way of showing your audience the real you is to take them through your day. Are you getting ready to go on a podcast? Post a couple of stories about what is involved with that. This is your opportunity to take them on more of your journey and help them really get to know the amazingness of you!

Whether you are going live, creating content or sharing stories, do it with the confidence that what you have to share matters! Everything you have to share matters to someone! A part of posting and sharing your day/life is believing in yourself, and this brings me to the 'Kick Ass Journal'.

One way I tackle those moments when my energy feels off is the 'Kick Ass Journal'. This is a journal that you write in when you feel amazing! When you are in the moment, and you have just worked with a client who achieved incredible results, write it down. Document it in your 'Kick Ass Journal.' First, write it down in the journal. Second, close your eyes and take in every aspect of the moment. What emotion? Sound? Smell? Write it all down. It is great to be able to see and reflect on your day through this journal. But the main purpose is to use it on those days when you feel like the sky is grey rather than blue. Pull out your 'Kick Ass Journal' and read how incredible you truly are, and as you read those moments when you felt radiant, close your eyes and take yourself back to that time. Then, before you open your eyes you say, 'I'm kick ass and I've got this!'

How would you present yourself through your content and in life if there was nothing holding you back? If you'd like to explore this more, please connect with me at Sparklewithnicole1@gmail.com.

Nicole Crowley

Nicole is a motivational speaker who focuses on empowering others to embrace their magic and bringing them to their self-healing/self-mastery capabilities. She helps people embody and embrace this through mindset work and quantum frequencies. Nicole focuses on spreading her message of SPARKLE and raising the collective consciousness! Spread Positivity Abundance Respect Kindness Love Everywhere! She and Amy Bingham, her twin flame, have created platforms to help people start their journey of spiritual awakening.

Nicole is passionate about bringing people's health back into their own hands, because she had the choice taken away from her. She was hit by a drunk driver seventeen years ago and sustained serious injuries. She was in rehabilitation for three-and-a-half years. She thought she was stuck in a place of darkness and pain forever, until she discovered the law of attraction. Even though her body was working against her, her mind never gave up! She wants to make sure everyone awakens to the power within themselves, so if they fall into darkness they will recognise they've always had the light within them, the creation power to bring themselves through!

Nicole is in the process of becoming certified as an emotional resonance clearing (ERC) practitioner. She will get her license in March 2022. ERC is a new modality that encompasses the five elements theory, naturopathic remedies and acupressure meridian clearing centres. Everything from Healy to ERC to mindset work that Nicole does is about empowering people to embrace their self-mastery/self-healing capabilities and, in turn, truly live with intention.

Work with Nicole:

Nicole is currently offering one-on-one sessions to help you find your true authentic self and the magic spark in what you do to share with world!

Special offer:

10% off any session booked with Nicole

Instagram: @SparklewNicole
Facebook: www.facebook.com/sparkleandglowfrequencies
LinkedIn: https://www.linkedin.com/in/%F0%9F%A6%8Bnicole-crowley%F0%9F%A6%8B-24833035
Email: Sparklewithnicole1@gmail.com

MASTERING YOUR SPIRITUAL MONEY GAME

Tools for decoding your money story, bringing yourself into alignment and making yourself an energetic match for everything you desire.

Leah Steele

The spiritual space is full of people who talk about alignment as though it is the only thing that needs to happen in order for you to live the life you desire. They reinforce beliefs that to live an abundant life you must be in alignment all of the time. But in the very next breath, they will blame being energetically blocked or 'out of alignment' as the reason they can't make the money they desire.

I call it bullshit.

First of all, NOBODY is in alignment all of the time. And you certainly don't need to be in alignment to make money.

Secondly, there are no blocks. They do not exist. You are not blocked from money. Blocks are a program and a construct. They are an obstacle created by YOU to hold YOURSELF back. The only thing that is blocking you is you.

The good news is that you also ultimately hold all the power in this game called life. And the sooner you start tapping into your personal power and realise that YOU are the most powerful creator in your reality, that you are the game master, the sooner you will be living the wildly abundant life you desire. I'll say it again ...YOU hold all the power. That means you have the ability, at any time, to become an energetic match with the small and large amounts of money you desire to have.

Let me let you in on a little secret: money actually isn't hard to make at all. You can make it whether you are in alignment or you aren't; the difference is that a whole other level of possibilities opens up for you when you align yourself with playing the game and step into your power!

So, if you are perceiving yourself to be blocked, it is because you are blocking yourself. You have positioned an obstacle between yourself and the thing you desire. Those 'blocks' exist for you to learn; they exist for you to look at where you are sabotaging yourself by sending mixed messages to the universe.

Nothing puts us in a stalemate the way sending mixed messages to the universe about what we want does:

'I want to be making twenty grand a month, but won't my grandmother think I'm extravagant?'

'I deserve to live in luxury, but won't people think that I believe I'm entitled?'

'I desire a seven-figure business, but is it greedy for me to want that?'

When you realise you are sending yourself and the universe mixed messages, and you commit to changing the behaviour, you will start to be able to identify those self-sabotaging patterns. Only then will you be able to turn them around, and get really honest with yourself about what you truly desire. By recognising the ways in which you are sabotaging your money game, you get to choose to shift so that you can fully, energetically back yourself. That energetic backing is what brings you into alignment with what you desire to manifest.

Do whatever it takes each moment of each day to shift back into alignment with your desires and the sky's the limit!

The above examples are perfect opportunities to look even deeper into the programming and conditioning that holds back the majority of humanity. Beliefs around greed, entitlement and extravagance are often built upon the idea that our world has limited resources.

Here is the actual truth: money is energy and energy is unlimited. That means that scarcity doesn't exist. It is a bullshit story fed to us to make us believe that by desiring more, we are taking away from someone else. We get triggered because we have been programmed and conditioned our entire lives to believe that if we want too much, we are greedy, and that somehow, by having more, we take away from the collective. That fear of causing harm or taking away from those who need money more than we do is enough to keep us in our place, playing small, and continually unable to manifest all that we deeply desire. And when we are playing small and staying in our place, we continue to operate like compliant commodities, serving the global financial agenda. That agenda is puppeteered by an elite few who control all of the resources of our planet and only have their own interests in mind. It's time to take our power back and shift the scales out of the favour for the few and into the favour for the collective.

Mastering Your Spiritual Money Game Tip: When you opt into the belief that money is energy and energy is unlimited, scarcity does not exist.

Something I see so often, especially with people who are already starting to make money, is that it becomes more difficult to align and make yourself an energetic match with larger sums of money. Ultimately, you use the same tools, but the alignment game is just happening on a different level. It requires more energetic support. It requires that we deconstruct the programming and beliefs … even of the things we have already looked at.

That is why wealth consciousness work and mastering your spiritual money game is forever work. It is a constant peeling back of the layers of the onion, and it is a continual shift back into alignment.

So how do you get into alignment?

The first thing is that you surrender the how. To be perfectly honest, I don't think anyone could figure out the 'how' behind how I have created what I have in my business. I do not believe even a team of forensic accountants could come in, look at my business, and be able to tell you how The Leah Steele Brand developed into a seven-figure business in such a short amount of time.

What I did, and what I continue to do, day after day, is bring myself back into a state of alignment with the impact that I desire to make in the world. I get very clear about what I desire and why I desire it. This is especially true when I have a specific financial goal I am working towards achieving. I decide how much money I want and get clear about how it is going to benefit me.

This tends to be where the majority of people stop the process. They get clear about why they want it for them and then just stop. This is the biggest mistake in manifestation. Especially for women. Women are service-based beings. We manifest so much more easily when what we desire to manifest not only benefits us, but also impacts the world. We are tribal beings by nature; that has always been our role. Somehow along the way, as we stepped into being these independent, financially driven women of the present age, we forgot that our goal is ultimately to care for humanity. Our goal is to care for our community and the collective.

For women, that is actually the magical secret to making money.

When we can figure out how having the money that we desire has an undeniable impact on humanity, nothing can stop us!

So do not stop at deciding how the money is going to benefit you. Get clear on how it is going to benefit your family, your extended family, your friends, your community, your extended community, your clients and, ultimately, ripple out and impact the whole world.

When we are properly resourced, we CAN and WILL take care of the whole village. And we have the power to move mountains.

But if we do not have that vision of how manifesting our desires is going to ripple out into the world, it is so much harder to achieve our desires. When I started going through this entire process every time I set a goal, things started happening for me much more quickly than they ever had before! But there is more to this process that will supercharge your manifestation abilities. Keep reading to learn the failproof tool I use to manifest everything I desire in my life.

People who believe in the law of attraction are going to disagree with what I have to say next:

I believe the negative repercussions of not showing up and doing the work you were meant to do in the world are equally, if not MORE important to explore than the positive ripple effect of your impact. What do I mean? As soon as you are crystal clear on the positive impact you will be able to make by manifesting your desires, explore the polar opposite. What happens if you don't make your goal or achieve your desires? How does that affect you, your family, extended family, your community and, ultimately, the world? What is the negative impact of you not showing up has on humanity? For me, achieving my goals frees men, women and children from financial slavery consciousness and empowers them to reclaim their financial destinies. When I don't show up, and I mean every single time that I allow my ego or my laziness to win and convince me that I can do something else instead, I perpetuate the enslavement of future generations. I condone the global financial elite using the beings of this planet as commodities, and I support building our global economy on the backs of the bodies of innocent men, women and children. THIS is the thing that helps me to get out of bed on the days I would much rather be resting. THIS is what motivates me to show up, even when I do not feel like it. THIS is what provides me with the energy to work twelve, fourteen and sixteen-hour days. On those days, it isn't about the positive impact. It is about the harm I would create if I didn't show up. Ultimately, this is how I manifest my desires rapidly and consistently.

If you have not figured out what the negative impact is of you not showing up and doing your purpose work in the world, get clear on that now. It's a powerful way to shift yourself back into alignment with your vision and your goals when the positive 'love and light' stuff isn't working.

It does not matter how small what you desire to manifest is. When you take the desire all the way out to its impact on the world, it is so much easier to manifest. When you are clear on that and continue to come back into alignment with that, the 'how' just presents itself. The right actions for you to take present themselves, day by day, as you bring yourself back to the vision you hold of the impact you desire to make.

Getting into alignment with your desires also means taking a good look at where you are spending your time and energy doing shit that is sucking the life out of you. One of the quickest ways of getting into alignment is to start saving your fucks for the things you actually desire to do. For everything else, delegate and hire out!

For example, I know I can do everything better than every single person that works for me. It is my business and so I just care about it more because it is my business. But there are so many things that are below my pay grade, so it just doesn't matter if I can do the job better because I have no business doing that job. It is so out of alignment for me to be spending the amount of time and energy on the things that my team does; that is why I have hired them. My job is to be the visionary of the business and stay focused on creating opportunities to be properly resourced to fulfill my divine mission work on this planet.

Something that worked very well for me in this department was that I started keeping a running list of the tasks I was doing that were sucking my soul dry. Then, every time the list reached ten tasks, I hired someone to do those things for me. Once I started doing that, my monthly revenue started increasing because I actually had the time to focus on income-generating activities. Instead of doing the stuff I hated, I was actually able to stay in my genius, which made me more money.

Look at what is taking you out of your zone of genius. What is making you time poor? What is below your pay grade? How much time are you spending doing things you don't want to do? I understand that there can be a fear around hiring people. But if you are making $1000 a month in your business, you should be paying someone at least $100 of that to do some of the tasks that are taking you away from income generating activities. What is it worth to free up five hours a week of your time?

For this to work, you don't get to just screw off those five hours. You take those five hours to focus on income-generating activities for your business or opening up additional streams of revenue for your family. If you started spending five hours more a week on income-generating activities, can you imagine what becomes possible in your business? In your life? I can tell you right now that five more hours in my business every week to spend on income-generating activities could easily double my income at this point!

I encourage you to try this activity and ask yourself: Where can

I create an extra five hours for myself by delegating or hiring out? If you desire to expand an existing business, create a new one, become financially free or are simply desiring to create abundance in all areas of your life, this is key. Hire the right people to take things off your plate so that you can do income-generating activities and stay in your lane of genius. That is what will ultimately make you successful.

Once you have freed up that time, get specific about what you are going to do with it as it pertains to alignment, and making yourself an energetic match for your desires. It is so important to track this all the way out. How would five more hours of income-generating activities benefit you, your family, extended family, community and, ultimately, the world? And on the flip side, how is not freeing up that time negatively impacting humanity?

Alignment may not be the key to making money, but it is the key to making an impact in the world. When you stay impact- and humanity-driven, that is when the money is energetically drawn to you. The wealthiest, most abundant and properly-resourced version of you has the power to effect massive change on this planet, so long as you keep coming back into alignment with your vision.

Stop reinforcing the programming and conditioning that you are blocked in some way. Decide to believe that you are the most powerful creator in your reality, and design the life of your dreams! You are so worthy and so deserving!

What's next? If you are ready to completely repattern your money story and fully embrace the spiritual money game, join me for my next round of my signature program Ouroboros: Quantum Wealth Repatterning. It is four months of deep introspective work that will change how you relate to money and increase your ability to manifest the wealth you deeply desire. While there is a mindset component to this work, this is NOT a 'Mindset Your Way to Millions' program. It is DEEP emotional clearing designed to deconstruct and neutralise conditioning and programming across multiple lifetimes, timelines and paradigms. This program is physical and spiritual in nature, working concurrently with the physical body (brain, organs and meridian systems) AND the spiritual body (mindset, chakra system and multi-dimensional timelines) so that you can call in all the PROSPERITY and ABUNDANCE you desire! The program uses my cutting-edge modality Emotional Resonance Clearing that is based on and inspired by the Chinese five element theory and philosophy, a body of wisdom and teaching that is more than 4000 years old. For more information visit my website: www.theleahsteele.com/ouroboros.

Leah Steele

Leah is the CEO of The Leah Steele Brand and the host of *The Wealth Witch Podcast*, a top wealth and entrepreneur podcast for women. She is a holistic wealth alchemist strategist, spiritual business coach, and creator of the Emotional Resonance Clearing modality.

Her purpose is to inspire and empower millions of people to wake up, repattern their wealth programming, and reclaim their divine right to be WEALTHY in all areas of their lives. The word wealthy comes from two words WELL and HEALTHY. Leah teaches holistic wealth as a means to simultaneously achieve infinite, divine and human potential.

Part of her divine mission work is to deconstruct the financial slavery consciousness that serves the global financial agenda. Her cutting edge wealth repatterning programs are paving the way to a new global wealth paradigm where economic freedom is the reality.

She coaches, mentors and guides those ready to create the abundantly wealthy lives and businesses they deeply desire. Her clients are wildly successful spiritual entrepreneurs on a mission to profoundly impact the planet.

Website: www.theleahsteele.com
Instagram: @theleahsteele

INTERNAL GROWTH AND QUANTUM LEAPING

Hinna Cassidy

No problem can be solved from the same level of consciousness that created it.

– Albert Einstein

When we take a look at our consciousness, it is formed from many layers. The most commonly known layer in our field is the physical body, our physical layer. We heal our physical layer by staying strong and fit. However, when we take a look at our entire bioenergetic field, we quickly realise that the health of our consciousness requires care and growth beyond physical matter.

When the feeling about ourselves turns negative (for example, disliking oneself), heavy 'clouds' are formed in our emotional layer. This vibration attracts lower vibrational people, events, circumstances and timelines into our life stream. This is the arena where some may fall into what we call a vicious repetitive cycle, never being able to catch a break.

How do we keep our emotional layer clean?

I once asked a hair stylist, who was having issues with some of the people around her, 'Can you tell me the difference between a cheap hair dye and a good quality one?'

To which she replied:

'Cheap hair dye will suffocate the hair strand. This will cause damage and, eventually, the hair will break. A good quality hair dye will colour the strand and still allow it to breathe, keeping it healthy and strong. This is due to the quality of the ingredients.'

It was then she had her 'aha' moment. She realised the importance of keeping good quality relationships close to her and keeping the others at a wide berth.

Keep well clear of toxic people and situations.

The average adult who has not been introduced to life stream or pathway of conscious internal growth, quite often presents with multiple energetic blocks in their system. This keeps them stuck, often repeating that particular life stream. As people adjust and move through their growth, it is important to remember that all situations that create emotional or energetic reactions are drawn towards them by the like-attracts-like vibration.

Keeping toxic people and situations in your life, is your vibration telling the universe 'I love this life of toxicity'. It does not serve you, beloved, these people and situations need to go.

Do not be afraid of shadow work

The health of your auric field is key to becoming a master at controlling each situation you place yourself into. There is one word everyone comes to know during their pathway of growth.

TRIGGERS

When you are triggered, someone has activated some deep scarring within your energy. Someone has activated a wound, causing a shadowed response. Quite often, your triggers are activated because of a situation that more than likely happened in your childhood. This can be from conditioning, belief systems and trauma. When a trigger activates, it is vital to drop straight into introspection, also known as mirror work. This is step one of my shadow release protocol when I have some really conditioned clients.

Tap into your current emotional reaction:

- frustration
- anger
- rage
- fear
- impatience
- anxiety

Where is this emotional reaction coming from? When did you first experience this (abandonment, poverty belief, lack of self-worth) feeling from?

An energetic wound is a painful episode from your past that has remained trapped in your system. Like a wound on the skin, you experience your first cut. You place a bandaid on top and leave it to heal; however, the tissue is never the same again. When you experience the first emotional traumatic episode of a wound, you place an energetic bandaid on top of it and bury the pain within. That pain could sit inside that wound for years until someone in high school challenges you, until a partner in our adulthood challenges you or until family challenges you over and over again.

Once that same emotional experience from that original wound is felt within your core, a trigger activates and out comes the shadow. Our shadows play a big role in how we drive life, how we enter into relationships, career and how we treat ourselves.

The more you react, the more you will experience this trigger, but with a different person. Once you find peace in a trigger, these lessons will fall away, and this wound will now be healed.

Remember, your thoughts drive your feelings, and when these become low vibrational, it compromises the health of your emotional layer. This is where we feel sad, heavy and unmotivated. When your auric field needs to raise its vibration, do not be afraid to give yourself some self-care days. Treat yourself with some yoga, meditation, diving, counselling, exercise, camping or reading that takes you into equilibrium. Confide in a trusted friend, do some tai chi, reiki, kintsugi, crafts, gardening, swimming, boxing or bake a cake for yourself. Buy yourself some flowers, go to a movie, go and sit by the sea and breathe. Take in the scenery, be present with nature. Drop into your heart, assess what needs light and breathe the light down into your heart space.

Never stop calling yourself out on your self-sabotaging habits.

A majority of my clients carry the same shadows. Quite often this comes from feelings of inadequacy, low confidence and abandonment. So many adults carry the 'mother' wound, 'father' wound, 'sister' wound or even the 'brother' wound. Mother wound is strong in those who hold great judgement over themselves or people. The mother wound of abandonment is one of the most common shadow reactions I see in my work.

Then we have the father wound. I usually see this in the form of either not speaking up as a father or being an abusive one. Verbal and physical abuse is not okay. If you do this, stop. If you allow this in your home, stop. This is a stubborn wound to remove because the victim of this wound is stuck in the belief that they must be the hunter and gatherer of the family in order to be a man. They must not show emotion. Healing this part of your patterns will bring you great love for yourself. Sister and brother wounds are quite often the result of bullying in school and carried on into the workforce. Whether you are receiver or sender, this wound creates very toxic habits.

Now, you have identified your wound, what next?

Acceptance.

Forgiveness.

Acknowledgement.

Making that psychological connection is already enough to help people start to see their worth, enough to give them the confidence to speak up and say 'I am', enough to help them start pulling themselves from self-destruction and into GROWTH.

The difference now is that current generations have the power to make an ancestral change for the generations to follow. This is why you are here; it is why I am here: we all want change.

What about the mental layer in our auric field? This is the arena where people hold toxic thought forms. They hold clouded judgement, and they compromise their own journey by staying in that comfort zone. The mental layer sits outside the physical and emotional layers. When you have some form of energy healing session, this is where your practitioner goes in order to see what is triggered, what is sluggish and what needs to go.

- victim consciousness
- unworthiness
- undeservingness
- addictions
- poverty consciousness
- self-destruction
- abandonment
- impatience
- intolerance
- conflict
- self-obsession

Sound familiar? These are what drive the negative thought forms in the mental layer. Healing this area of your field comes from positive thought creation.

How can you begin to change your mindset?

Affirmations: Say them, write them, paint them! Start young, share with children, and make a habit of utilising these in your everyday life.

Journaling: Such a powerful tool of mindset and manifestation training.

Self-Care days: A hands down MUST for a healthy feeling of self-worth.

Heavy metal detox: Great for the mind, great to clear the junk, great for the body.

Cut out sugar: Your behaviour dramatically changes when sugar is cut out of your diet or reduced.

Speak from the heart, not from your mind.

Treat yourself how you would treat your dearest.

Admire yourself the way you admire looking up at the milky way.

Treat and talk to others the way you wish to be treated.

Keep on top of shifting your perspective, always.

Last of all …

Shadow work: Embrace it; embody it.

Internal growth will take you through the depths of discomfort, which is why people usually give up, reapply a bandaid and push their wounded emotions deeper into their bioenergetic field, waiting for the next trigger.

Know your worth. When you fall into alignment, your body will be charged, your ego excited and your soul feels joy, or, perhaps, your body is bubbly, your ego happy and your soul is serene. This is mindset change; this is the feeling and the accomplishment of internal growth and up levelling. When I see my clients turn that corner, that 'aha' moment sets in – it really melts my heart. There is no going back. When you do the internal work, you experience the rewards; and when you find your worth, there is no stopping you!

Our feelings are driven by either the body, the ego, or the soul. They will either be aligned or misaligned. The trick is being able to track your personal emotional state. For example, when someone is misaligned, their body is weary, the ego may feel tense and the soul sad. Some bodies are exhausted, their ego in a state of resentment and the soul is left feeling withdrawn.

Hara Healing

Hara is the first step, the last step, and the only step in the pathway of liberation. It is the state of non-action supported and held by intention. Sedentary living, poor eating habits, lack of purpose, lack of drive, poor breathing and posture all contribute to poor hara. A person's hara can be split. This means the flow of energy through their vertical power column becomes distorted. This throws off the entire system, as all of the energetics are built around strong, healthy functioning hara. Split hara is common when someone has a split intention. For example, an aspirant might want to leave their job or partner, but another part of them is drawn back to the feeling of being needed at work or home. Thus, they are split by their intent of wanting to leave and subconscious feeling of being needed. This can create split hara, which throws their energy out of balance.

Here are some personal tools I like to add for everyday growth:

Colour Therapy, Chanting, Breathwork and Sound Healing

Your auric field expands and flows with the most loving and highest vibrations. Filling your vibe with breathwork, sound, colour, chanting and Hara healing will deliver a stronger change in the strength of your journey.

Frequency Therapy Healy Device Cycles

- GOLD CYCLE – release, being, pure
- MENTAL – emotional balance, inner unity, wellbeing, soul
- JOB – exhaustion, positive thoughts, stress
- DEEP CYCLE – digest all, breath of life, female kidneys
- PROTECTION – all protection cycles

Aromatherapy and Homeopathy

- lavender
- peppermint
- orange
- frankincense
- myrrh
- Siberian fir
- aconite
- lycopodium
- Nat-mur
- sulphur
- Lachesis

Romiromi and Mirimiri

An ancient Maori technique which physically forces ancestral traumas and attachments out of our body. It is not massage; it is a unique sacred experience, and it is worth all it has to offer.

Moving forward, I challenge you to take the step into a more sovereign version of yourself.

Start small. Start by writing a simple goal in your journal twice a week and read some affirmations. Take yourself to a massage, and honour yourself in connection with some positive friends. Remember, each day is a fresh opportunity for growth.

The ball is in your court, Beloved.

Hinna Cassidy

Hinna Cassidy is of Irish and Maori descent. She was born and raised in the Pilbara, Western Australia, where her parents settled after migrating from New Zealand in 1976. Hinna predominantly worked in masculine, heavy haulage industries, however she was called into her healing business journey in 2015. This is where Hinnaz Alchemy was birthed. This movement was a creation to help other women find their confidence to walk away from situations of domestic violence.

However, it was soon discovered that this movement would quickly take on a bigger role and become an empowerment business for both men and women. Hinna went through initiations and teachings of the bioenergetic field and soon starting teaching people how to keep their space clear and change their mindset on a really deep level.

Hinna works alongside people from all walks of life, in a non-judgement space, who are ready to start releasing generational and ancestral conditioning, also known as shadows and wounds. Hinna loves to facilitate ceremonial cacao circles, group meditations and sound healing. Groups are her absolute specialty.

Hinna works professionally within the spiritual industry and specialises in trauma. She is an ancient Maori healing romiromi practitioner, holistic hypnotherapist (specialising in trauma), meditation coach, shamanic healer, colour mirrors practitioner, psychic medium, reiki master, empowerment coach, light code facilitator and sound healing therapist.Work with Hinna:

If you feel called to start taking your power back and really step into the full ownership of your body, your life and your emotional self, Hinnaz Alchemy welcomes you.

Website: www.hinnazalchemy.com
Instagram: @hinna_cassidy
Facebook: Hinemoa Cassidy

STEPPING INTO YOUR SOVEREIGN LEADER ENERGY

Finding sovereignty through unconditional love and self-mastery.

Soraya XXxO

As I sat up in bed one morning (yuck, this is sounding like a cheesy novel, I promise it's not), I looked around my room and took note of every little thing I had accumulated over forty-three years. And I mean everything. I saw clothes with tags still on them, shoes, boots from every designer, handbags, jewellery, furniture, art. I lacked no THING. In everyone else's eyes, I had it all: the beautiful family, house, cars and my own business. I asked myself that morning: Why do I feel unhappy, alone, unfulfilled? And that's when a little voice in my head told me, 'Soraya, happiness comes from experiences, not THINGS.' I soon realised it was not only experiences I was in search of, I was looking for myself.

I no longer wanted to identify as Soraya from BraBarBoutique, Xander's mom, or someone's wife (or ex-wife). I wanted to find ME in my full sovereignty. I needed to step into my power: the power that screamed SORAYA that I had lost somewhere within me! Not one that my business gave me or that motherhood bestowed on me (not that those powers didn't serve their purpose or were terrible things).

What is sovereignty? What did this look like for me? How do I bring back my Soraya-power? I decided the answer was to sell all my belongings, pack my life into two suitcases and move to Bali. I had to get away from my everyday routine. I had to go far enough away that I couldn't cry for help and have someone on the next flight out. I had to go where the only thing that could distract me was my fear of not finding Soraya.

Deciding to leave your life is not an easy decision to make. Are people going to think I was running? Are they going to think my business failed? Am I going to be judged for going through my second divorce? Am I a bad mother because I won't be there to spend the holidays with my son? Will my friends think I am selfish because I am doing me now, with no fucks for what they believe? Yes, to all of these questions. Friends and family judged me every which way, but I did not care! And there it was. I was stepping into my sovereignty and empowering myself without even realising it.

I needed to do what my soul called me to do. And every fibre of my soul said yes to Bali. I was respecting and honouring my space first and the space of others second, and that upset people. It honestly pissed some people off: friends and family who I love dearly. I've been called selfish, stupid and reckless, to name a few. But if they love me, they will continue to love me. I couldn't be afraid of them not loving me, because I would be stepping outside of my sovereignty again if I was.

This brings me to the number one thing I believe we must do to step into our sovereignty. We must have unconditional love – unconditional love for ourselves, so in return, we can love others unconditionally and lead in complete integrity.

When you love yourself unconditionally, it won't matter to you if people think you are selfish, stupid or reckless. You create your boundaries, and you refuse to settle for anything that does not serve your soul. You are aligning with what you need to do so as to do what YOU need to do. You begin to disentangle yourself from all the manipulated versions of love that we have all been taught (a whole chapter in itself). As soon as you care what other people think of you, you no longer love yourself unconditionally. You are limiting yourself to what other people think of you; therefore, you are giving up your sovereignty.

Had I listened to the naysayers and cared what people were saying about me moving to Bali, I would have been loving myself conditionally to appease others' opinions. I would have stayed home and continued to live the redundant routine that kept me out of being authentic with who I am and who I want to be. It is in that space of self-love that your leader energy happens; it flows. You are not motivated by fear but by love. You cannot give or bring the correct leader energy if you are not doing it in complete love.

Sovereignty allows others around you to honour their soul and live in their freedom. In return, you will step fully into leadership because you are guiding them to be ultimately themselves and not live in your paradigm. Sovereignty allows all to be who they are genuinely called here to be. Sovereignty mothers sovereignty.

It is not easy. I've been called all sorts of names. I received very hurtful comments from family and friends because I have held my boundaries and chosen to love what I love and have kept on a path that makes me happy. I have been ostracised and accused of many things that are not true. But there is no better feeling than knowing I have fully trusted myself. I have put myself first and have stopped making myself wrong, stopped questioning myself. I've made it my art to trust my inner voice. My SHE-instinct is always correct, and I stand in full sovereignty with her.

Thoughts are little love notes from the universe. This is where the second step to becoming sovereign comes into play. You have to be so in tune with your inner self. When you have thoughts or feelings, these are whispers from the universe to guide you to the step you should be taking next. These whispers are our intuition telling us, 'I know what you need. I know what's best for you.' It's that inner voice that tells you that you are no longer in a space that serves you: when you feel those goosebumps on the back of your neck, you cannot spit out your words because they're choked up in your throat, or you feel a pit in your gut because you are uneasy. However your inner self speaks to you, it is not a coincidence. Your soul is trying to tell you something. Trust your soul, unconditionally!

Most of us ignore these inner feelings and thoughts. When I lay in my bed and cried myself to sleep (please tell me I'm not the only one who has done this), I would nudge these thoughts and feelings away. I would say to myself that I overthink too much, that I am just too sensitive, that I need to toughen up and stop being such a wussy, that I'm just drunk, that it's not a pit in my stomach, I just need to use the washroom, that I'm stupid and insecure and nobody likes stupid and insecure, and on until I had convinced myself that my thoughts and feelings were irrelevant and didn't matter, and I was going to conform to what my family, friends or other people thought I was or should be doing instead of loving myself unconditionally and knowing that I know what is best for me. Loving myself unconditionally means trusting myself. Every feeling. Every thought. Every emotion. Every breath.

To love yourself unconditionally, you need to know thyself.

What is it to know thyself?

To know thyself is daily work. It's not just doing yoga, meditating and going to the spa and having facials and mani–pedis. However, all those things are lovely, too. Your mind, your body, your emotions, everything about you is evolving daily. You never stay the same. And that is okay too! We have this preconceived notion that if we feel like something one day, we can't change our minds the next day. We think if we quit something (eating meat, for example), we have to quit forever. There have been many instances where I have felt the need to stop drinking for a while. And then, two weeks later (or however long), I decide I want a drink. And that is okay. It is my body. My body will tell me what I need or don't need. Not my bestie. Not society. Not my man. ME.

We need to learn to know, without a shadow of a doubt, what serves us, what our body and soul says yes and no to, to know intimately what our body and soul's desires are, and what makes us tick or what makes us sick. Be comfortable enough in your skin to admit if you like something or don't. And this goes for all things, including pleasures or discomforts in (out or around) the bedroom. Many of us are unsatisfied because we are too 'shy' to admit when our body has inner urges and we are turned on. We want more but can't admit it. Or we don't want to hurt someone's feelings because they're not doing it right, so we suffer through it and get nothing from it (this is a whole series in itself!).

Let's talk about what we put in our bodies. I have recently taken a six-week journey of self-mastery called the Inner Alchemy. These six weeks just touched the basics. How can I master myself if I don't know what my spleen is or where my spleen is located, and which emotions derive from my spleen (and this is just one organ amongst the many)? Do I know myself if I don't even 'know the vessel I'm walking around in'? (Thank you, Michelle Patrick, for the quote.)

I have learnt to stop wasting my time doing things just for shits and giggles. I have come to a place in my life when time is precious. I now ask myself, 'How does this serve me? Will this add quality to my day, or am I doing this to appease someone else?' My body and soul will give me the answer every time without fail. Don't get me wrong; I have suffered from fear of missing out (FOMO) like I think most people do. And every time I have listened to my FOMO (ego), I have regretted wasting time doing things that did not serve my purpose. At the end of the day, if you really have to ask, isn't the answer usually 'NO'?

I have touched briefly on how to step into your sovereignty through unconditional love for yourself, but we could write a whole book about this subject in all reality. There are many ways to be sovereign, and your sovereign may, and probably does, look different from mine. And that is okay! Because you loving yourself unconditionally takes you out of my paradigm and into your own. And I love you for that. Lead from your heart and not from mine.

Let's bring this full circle now.

Sovereignty derives from loving myself unconditionally. To love me unconditionally, I will be fully aligned and trust my mind, my thoughts, my body, my feelings and my emotions, without a shadow of a doubt. To trust me 100 per cent, I will 'know thyself'. To know myself, I will practise self-mastery daily. Daily self-mastery leads to more confidence in trusting myself because I am honouring the authentic me, resulting in dropping judgment on myself, therefore loving myself unconditionally.

Self-mastery tips that are suggestions, not law.

These tips are easy when you do them, but it is a daily practice. As I said, we change daily; therefore, we should be checking in with our mind, body, and soul, DAILY! When I use the term 'ME', I refer to my body, mood, soul, appetite, mind, and everything that has to do with ME. Here are four of my faves, although this is just touching the base.

- Journaling is vital. I keep tabs on my bleed cycle, so I know where the moon is and how this will affect me (MoonX is an excellent app for this). I write down what I eat, so I know how certain foods affect me. I write down events that affect my mood and dive into why it has affected me, which goes for positive and adverse events.

~ Speaking my truth (this is a difficult one for me). Saying no when I mean no and yes when I mean yes. Participating when I want to and sitting it out if I am too tired or I simply don't want to do it. Admitting if I am comfortable or uncomfortable in a situation or with a particular person, place or thing.

~ Asking myself daily if what I did yesterday still serves me today. If it doesn't, I change it. For instance, I cut out cheeseburgers for a minute, but now my body craves it, so I'm going to eat it, guiltless! Or, I liked F45 for a couple of months, and now I want to try Orange Theory. You can change your mind whenever it serves your greater good or just for the hell of it! It is up to you!

~ Making love to the person you love best, and yes, that better be you. Unconditionally. Masturbation is a thing, and if this makes you cringe, you have a lot of self-mastery to do.

When you surrender to your soul because you 'know thyself 'and 'love thyself' unconditionally, the all-knowing, all-powerful, you are guiding you! THAT is when you step into your Sovereign Leader Energy!

I love speaking to women and young ladies. If you'd like to book me for an event you can visit my website: www.thesorayaxxxo.com

XXxO

Soraya XXxO

Soraya is a self-motivated, free spirit who believes life happens for us, not to us.

She was born a Utah native and recently relocated to Bali, Indonesia. After her second divorce, giving up her business and having a son who is now an adult, she decided it was time to face her fears and go out on her own.

Having owned her own lingerie business for the last ten years (and previously working in the beauty industry for fifteen years), she was given the opportunity to work daily with women in a very intimate setting. It made her very aware of women's insecurities and where they derive from.

Also, opening her eyes to how much women really need the camaraderie of other women. This put her in a position of becoming very passionate about empowering women by living and leading through integrity and by example.

In 2019 she served a year as Mrs Salt Lake City. This gave her a whole other insight into women that come from the pageant world. That in itself is a whole different breed of insecurities. She was reminded, yet again, how much women really empower each other when they stay vital to their womanhood and sistership. She has committed herself to always connecting with women and bringing them together to build a network of sovereign women who want to embrace the world to guide them to their highest being.

Philanthropy work is essential to her. She founded the Night of Empowerment charity gala that enables breast cancer survivors to live fully beyond breast cancer by providing no-cost weekend retreats. She is always trying to find ways to help her community.

While in Bali, she has coached with Les Brown to become a motivational speaker. She enjoys speaking to women but also adores young ladies and children. She likes to spread her message: 'Fail fast, fail often, fail forward.'

She believes she is in the most critical learning phase of her life and looks forward to sharing her journey along with her life lessons as she goes.

Websites: www.thesorayaxxxo.com &
https://www.healy.shop/de/partner/?partnername=sori garfield
Instagram: Instagram.com/TheSorayaXX/
Facebook: https://www.facebook.com/soraya.garfield

FINAL WORD

Tracey Jewel

I came together with these amazing wellness experts knowing that this book, the journal and the intention cards are going to change lives.What brought us together is a common passion for living a high vibrational life and connecting through an amazing frequency device called Healy.

We have each taken the best learnings and wisdom and distilled it down into this book, through the vehicle of Healy and wellness that we know will truly change the trajectory of the lives and businesses of our readers.

We are committed to introducing the Healy device and bringing Healy's vision to life in one million homes.

So what is Healy?

Healy is a new wearable device, designed by a German quantum physicist/Buddhist monk, that analyses your frequency via a quantum sensor and then delivers customised frequency programs through a micro-current, to promote bio-energetic balance, vitality and overall wellbeing.

The Healy offers over 120 programs with 144,000 different frequencies, to harmonise your body, your organs, your mental state, your emotional being and your soul wellbeing.

This is the time to take action on all those ideas, goals and dreams you've been desiring and envisioning and create momentum with a likeminded tribe – with us!

Find your frequency

We would love for you to experience a free remote frequency session with Healy.

Please visit www.upself.com.au/healy to book your free remote frequency session today!

Disclaimer:

Healy is designed to harmonise your bioenergetic field and enhance recovery, vitality and wellbeing, not to cure, treat, mitigate, diagnose or prevent disease. The information on these pages is for reference and educational purposes only. It should not be treated as a substitute for professional medical advice, diagnosis or treatment. You should always seek such advice from a qualified medical professional.

We are a collection of independent brand partners and are not part of Healy Corporate.

Healy World, with the advice of its medical advisory board, allows its members to only make claims that are contained in company materials meant for public distribution. Please contact the company concerning any claims about which you have questions.

DECODING THE WELLNESS MANTRA

Reflection Journal + Intention Cards

Decoding the Wellness Mantra Reflection Journal – $26.99

Manifest a high-frequency lifestyle with help from this self-guided journal.

Embracing positivity is essential when you want to elevate your life and business. Learn how to raise your vibration one journal entry at a time.

Intention cards – $26.99

This collection of intention cards provides the boost you need to think positively, keep your goals in mind, release negativity and create the life you want.

The companion book and reflection journal provide a more detailed roadmap. The intention cards are designed for you to take the inspired action steps necessary to move forward and improve your personal and business life with simple inspirational affirmations.